CTHULHU CALLS

There are primeval forces that were worshipped and summoned long before the creation of the Qabala. They are the Ancient Ones of the Sumerian faith, and they live on in the magick of Aleister Crowley and the mythos of H. P. Lovecraft. They wait beyond the Gate, ready to rule the Earth once again . . .

This long-lost sorceror's handbook contains incantations and conjurations, exorcisms and bindings. But they are not to be used lightly. We can only guess what horrible fate prevented Abdul Alhazred from completing this Book of the Black Earth. And remember, there are no effective banishings for the forces invoked in the NECRONOMICON.

> "The NECRONOMICON'S magick is nothing to fool with and it may expose you to psychological forces with which you cannot cope. Remember, if you tinker with the incantations, *you were warned*."
>
> *Fate Magazine*

Necronomicon Books

THE NECRONOMICON
NECRONOMICON SPELLBOOK
THE GATES OF THE NECRONOMICON

THE NECRONOMICON

Edited with an Introduction by

Simon

AVON BOOKS

AVON BOOKS
An Imprint of HarperCollins*Publishers*
195 Broadway
New York, NY 10007

Copyright © 1977 by Schlangekraft, Inc.
Library of Congress Catalog Card Number: 79-56778
ISBN: 0-380-75192-5
www.avonbooks.com

Designed by Studio 31
Typography by Feint Type
Artwork by Khem Set Rising

First Avon Books Printing: March 1980

Avon Trademark Reg. U.S. Pat. Off. and in Other Countries, Marca Registrada, Hecho en U.S.A.
HarperCollins® is a trademark of HarperCollins Publishers Inc.

Printed in the U.S.A.

80 79 78 77 76 75

Dedication

On the One Hundredth Anniversary

of the Nativity of the Poet

ALEISTER CROWLEY

1875 - 1975

Ad Meiorum Cthulhi Gloriam

ACKNOWLEDGEMENTS

THE EDITOR would like to thank all of the people whose cooperation and dedication to unspeakable horrors has made this book possible. First, our thanks go to that nameless monk who presented us with the original ms., who has since disappeared. Second, to that ever-changing staff of translators who performed a most distasteful and oft'times unsatisfying task: to Ms. I. Celms, Ms. N. Papaspyrou, Mr. Peter Levenda, Mr. X. and Mr. Y. Third, to Ms. J. McNally, whose thorough knowledge and understanding of Craft folklore aided the Editor in assuming a proper perspective towards this Work. Fourth, to Mr. J. Birnbaum, who aided in some of the preliminary practical research concerning the powers of the Book, and its dangers. Fifth, to Mr. L.K. Barnes, who dared to tempt the awesome wrath of the Ancient Ones, risking unspeakable eldritch horrors, in supporting the publication of this arcane treatise. Sixth, to all those patient Pagans and Friends of the Craft who waited, and waited for the eventual publication of this tome with baited breath . . . and something on the stove. Seventh, and perhaps most importantly, to Herman Slater of the Magickal Childe (nee Warlock Shop), whose constant encouragement and eternal kvetching was material to the completion of this Work.

And, finally, to the Demon PERDURABO, without whose help the presentation of this Book would have been impossible.

Blessed Be!

TABLE OF CONTENTS

INTRODUCTION

The NECRONOMICON

PREFACE TO THE SECOND EDITION

THERE ARE THREE major individuals who must share the credit for the astonishingly good reception the NECRON-OMICON has enjoyed over the last two years since its publication. L.K. Barnes was lured into the Magickal Childe bookstore in Manhattan one day by an incarnated thoughtform we may only refer to by his initials, B.A.K. Both were in search of some casual amusement from the slightly distorted version of the supernatural intelligence-dissemination that usually took place on those premises. L.K. Barnes, publisher of this tome, has probably come to regret ever setting foot or tentacle inside those clammy precincts, for the crazed proprietor of that institution commenced to wave before him the manuscript copy of this book, thereby securing his soul forever in the service of the Elder Gods.

Needless to say, L.K.—a longtime pilgrim in the search for the genuine NECRONOMICON which he knew, since childhood, really existed—was suitably impressed. Shocked, actually. He asked to see the dubious personality who claimed responsibility for the editing and general research work that went into the volume.

This exotic individual, Simon by name, appeared suddenly one day at the living quarters of L.K. Barnes attired in a beret, a suit of some dark, fibrous material, and an attache case which contained—besides correspondence from various Balkan embassies and a photograph of the F-104 fighter being crated up for shipment to Luxembourg—additional material on the NECRONOMICON which proved his *bona fides*. Also at that meeting was the third member of the Unholy Trinity, James Wasserman of Studio 31 who—according to a South American cult leader—died during the last year, but who has been able with assistance from the Stone of the Wise and certain of the formulae in this book, to go on about his business like unto a living man.

With Simon's manuscript, Barnes' occult vision and aesthetic scruples, and Wasserman's production experience and tireless labor, the abhorred NECRONOMICON began to take shape and the first edition smote the stands on December 22, 1977—the ancient pagan feast of Yule, the winter solstice.

Yet, not without a number of bizarre occurrences that more than once threatened the lives, the sanity, and the astral bodies of the three individuals most deeply involved.

Jim Wasserman was subjected to what we may vaguely refer to as "poltergeist" activity during the time he worked on production and design aspects of the book. A room which, for certain loathsome purposes, was always kept locked was found one day to have been opened—*from the inside*. In the same building, just below his loft, the typesetters were set upon by swarms of rats. The discovery of a small Hindu idol that had been lost signalled the end to the plague, and the rats disappeared.

Simon usually lives in fear of his life, for reasons that do not always have to do with the NECRONOMICON. However, he has been subject to constant surveillance by the Ancient Ones as they await the one slip, the single misstep, that will provide for them the entry they earnestly desire into this world.

L.K. Barnes, on the other hand, has had no rest whatever from the signals and messages from the extraterrestrial intelligences that were the overseers and the guardians of the book's publication. He has been plagued by an unremitting chain of numerological events which he cannot ignore. The predominance of the numbers 13,333,555,666 and others too arcane to bear mentioning have made his life a demonstration (read, demon-stration) of Jungian synchronicity patterns. Also, his printing of the beautiful, full-color *Denderah Zodiac* on the first anniversary of the NECRONOMICON's publication in 1978 precipitated a rash of UFO sightings in Australia and New Zealand—in which one pilot has disappeared.

Bizarre occurrences and humorous coincidences aside for

the moment, the NECRONOMICON has caused changes in the consciousness of those people most intimately involved with it, as well as many strangers who simply bought the book through the mail or at their bookstore. Judging by the letters we have received in the last two years, these changes have been startling. Many have found the books' magick to work, and work extremely well. Others, having once attempted certain of the rituals, felt compelled to retire from the occult "scene" for lengthy periods of time. The mere fact that the books was generally considered never to have existed—and then found to exist after all—is itself a powerful psychic influence. A fantasy come true. A dream realized in waking life. The quest for a lifetime search come to an end. The ultimate Book of Spells. The Godfather of Grimoires.

Therefore it is with awe, and with something akin to dread, that I address this second edition to the courageous reader of the NECRONOMICON. The Beast has told us, "I am the warrior Lord of the Forties: the Eighties cower before me, & are abased." (AL, III:46) This edition of the NECRONOMICON is scheduled for early delivery in January-February 1980, making it possibly the first occult book of the Eighties. A herald of doom? Or a harbinger of fate?

Since the publication of this book in December, 1977, the ancient forces of erstwhile victory have been banging and clamoring at the Gates. December 1977 was the middle of the killing spree of the .44 calibre killer, known to the press as the Son of Sam, who was motivated—according to recent reports—by membership in a satanic cult in Yonkers. Several months after the capture of David Berkowitz in 1978, nearly one thousand people killed themselves in Guyana at the orders of a crazed religious leader. Several months after that, the leader of a mystical Islamic sect seized power in Iran and—at the time of this writing—is calling for a Holy War against the Infidel.

There is evidence that every New Age witnesses a baptism by fire. Christians and Muslims are turning on each other and themselves; Israel is once again in serious jeopardy; Buddhism is being eradicated in Southeast Asia as it was in Tibet.

The Ancient Ones, Lords of a time before memory, are being drawn by the smell of confusion and the hysteria and mutual hatred of the primitive life-forms on this planet: human beings. Unless the Gates are secured against attack, unless humanity awakens to both the real danger and the real potential for evolution . . .

Well, the vision of the Mad Arab—ancestor of the Muslim princes so much in the news in 1979/80—is one, certainly of terror. The discovery of this book, however, like the discovery of the typesetters' idol, may be the key, the link in our defence against the possible Enemy awaiting us, Outside. Events of the last two years have shown us that the book is also an amulet, a protective shield, that guards its own from the machinations of evil. Extraterrestrial or primevally elemental, alien beings or subconscious repressions, they are powerless against us if we consider deeply the message of this book, and take the seeming ranting of the Arab at face value for what they are: a warning, a weapon, and a wisdom. With these three we enter the New Age of the Crowned and Conquering Child, Horus, not in a slouch towards Bethlehem, but born within us at the moment we conquer the lurking fear in our own souls.

New York, N.Y.
December, 1979

"Our work is therefore historically authentic; the rediscovery of the Sumerian Tradition."

—Aleister Crowley

INTRODUCTION

IN THE MID-1920'S, roughly two blocks from where the Warlock Shop once stood, in Brooklyn Heights, lived a quiet, reclusive man, an author of short stories, who eventually divorced his wife of two years and returned to his boyhood home in Rhode Island, where he lived with his two aunts. Born on August 20, 1890, Howard Phillips Lovecraft would come to exert an impact on the literary world that dwarfs his initial successes with *Weird Tales* magazine in 1923. He died, tragically, at the age of 46 on March 15, 1937, a victim of cancer of the intestine and Bright's Disease. Though persons of such renown as Dashiell Hammett were to become invovled in his work, anthologizing it for publication both here and abroad, the reputation of a man generally conceded to be the "Father of Gothic Horror" did not really come into its own until the past few years, with the massive re-publication of his works by various houses, a volume of his selected letters, and his biography. In the July, 1975, issue of *The Atlantic Monthly*, there appeared a story entitled "There Are More Things", written by Jorge Luis Borges, "To the memory of H.P. Lovecraft". This gesture by a man of the literary stature of Borges is certainly an indication that Lovecraft has finally ascended to his rightful place in the history of American literature, nearly forty years after his death.

In the same year that Lovecraft found print in the pages of *Weird Tales*, another gentleman was seeing *his* name in print; but in the British tabloid press.

NEW SINISTER REVELATIONS OF ALEISTER CROWLEY read the front page of the *Sunday Express*. It concerned testimony by one of the notorious magician's former followers (or, actually, the wife of one of his followers) that Crowley had been responsible for the death of her husband, at the Abbey of Thelema, in Cefalu, Sicily. The bad press, plus the imagined threat of secret societies, finally forced Mussolini to deport the Great Beast from Italy. Tales of horror filled the pages of the newspapers in England for weeks and months to come: satanic rituals, black masses, animal sacrifice, and even human sacrifice, were reported—or blatantly lied about. For, although many of the stories were simply not true or fanciful exaggeration, one thing was certain: Aleister Crowley was a Magician, and one of the First Order.

Born on October 12, 1875, in England—in the same county as Shakespeare—Edward Alexander Crowley grew up in a strict Fundamentalist religious family, members of a sect called the "Plymouth Brethren". The first person to call him by that Name and Number by which he would become famous (after the reference in the Book of Revelation), "The Beast 666", was his mother, and he eventually took this appellation to heart. He changed his name to Aleister Crowley while still at Cambridge, and by that name, plus "666", he would never be long out of print, or out of the newspapers. For he believed himself to be the incarnation of a god, an Ancient One, the vehicle of a New Age of Man's history, the Aeon of Horus, displacing the old Age of Osiris. In 1904, he had received a message, from what Lovecraft might have called "out of space", that contained the formula for a New World Order, a new system of philosophy, science, art and religion, but this New Order had to begin with the fundamental part, and common denominator, of all four: Magick.

In 1937, the year Lovecraft died, the Nazis banned the occult lodges of Germany, notable among them two organizations which Crowley had supervised: the A∴A∴ and the O.T.O., the latter of which he was the elected head in England, and the former which he founded himself. There are those who believe that Crowley was somehow, magickally, responsible for the Third Reich, for two reasons: one, that the emergence of New World Orders generally seems to instigate holocausts and, two, that he is said to have influenced the mind of Adolf Hitler. While it is almost certain that Crowley and

Hitler never met, it is known that Hitler belonged to several occult lodges in the early days after the First War; the symbol of one of these, the *Thule Gesellschaft* which preached a doctrine of Aryan racial superiority, was the infamous Swastika which Hitler was later to adopt as the Symbol of the Third Reich. That Crowley only despised Nazism in all its forms, however, is evident in many of his writings, notably the essays written in the late 'Thirties. Crowley seemed to regard the Nazi phenomenon as a Creature of Christianity, in it's anti-Semitism and severe moral restrictions concerning its adherents, which lead to various types of lunacies and "hang-ups" that characterised many of the Reich's leadership. Yet, there can be perhaps little doubt that the chaos which engulfed the world in those years was prefigured, and predicted, in Crowley's *Liber AL vel Legis*; the *Book of the Law*.

The Mythos and the Magick

We can profitably compare the essence of most of Lovecraft's short stories with the basic themes of Crowley's unique system of ceremonial Magick. While the latter was a sophisticated psychological structure, intended to bring the initiate into contact with his higher Self, via a process of individuation that is active and dynamic (being brought about by the "patient" himself) as opposed to the passive depth analysis of the Jungian adepts, Lovecraft's *Cthulhu Mythos* was meant for entertainment. Scholars, of course, are able to find higher, ulterior motives in Lovecraft's writings, as can be done with any manifestation of Art.

Lovecraft depicted a kind of Christian Myth of the struggle between opposing forces of Light and Darkness, between God and Satan, in the *Cthulhu Mythos*. Some critics may complain that this smacks more of the Manichaen heresy than it does of genuine Christian dogma; yet, as a priest and former monk, I believe it is fair to say that this dogma is unfortunately very far removed from the majority of the Faithful to be of much consequence. The idea of a War against Satan, and of the entities of Good and Evil having roughly equivalent Powers, is perhaps best illustrated by the belief, common among the Orthodox churches of the East, in a personal devil as well as a personal angel. This concept has been amplified by the Roman Catholic Church to such an extent—perhaps subconsciously—that a missal in the Editor's possession contains an engraving for the Feast of St. Andrew, Apostle, for November 30, that bears the legend "Ecce Qui Tollis Peccata Mundi"—Behold Him Who Taketh Away The Sins of the World—and the picture above it is of the atomic bomb!

Basically, there are two "sets" of gods in the *mythos*: the *Elder Gods*, about whom not much is revealed, save that they are a stellar Race that occasionally comes to the rescue of man, and which corresponds to the Christian "Light"; and the *Ancient Ones*, about which much is told, sometimes in great detail, who correspond to "Darkness". These latter are the Evil Gods who wish nothing but ill for the Race of Man, and who constantly strive to break into our world through a Gate or Door that leads from the Outside, In. There are certain people, among us, who are devotees of the Ancient Ones, and who try to open the Gate, so that this evidently repulsive organization may once again rule the Earth. Chief among these is *Cthulhu,* typified as a Sea Monster, dwelling in the Great Deep, a sort of primeval Ocean; a Being that Lovecraft collaborator August Derleth wrongly calls a "water elemental". There is also *Azathoth*, the blind idiot god of Chaos, *Yog Sothot*, Azathoth's partner in Chaos, *Shub Niggurath*, the "goat with a thousand young", and others. They appear at various times throughout the stories of the Cthulhu Mythos in frightening forms, which test the strength and resourcefulness of the protagonists in their attempts to push the hellish Things back to whence they came. There is an overriding sense of primitive fear and cosmic terror in those pages, as though man is dealing with something that threatens other than his physical safety: his very spiritual nature. This horror-cosmology is extended by the frequent appearance of the Book, NECRONOMICON.

The NECRONOMICON is, according to Lovecraft's tales, a volume written in Damascus in the Eighth Century, A.D., by a person called the "Mad Arab", Abdul Alhazred. It must run roughly 800 pages in length, as there is a reference in one of the stories concerning some lacunae on a page in the 700's. It had been copied and reprinted in various languages— the story goes—among them Latin, Greek and English. Doctor Dee, the Magus of Elizabethan fame, was supposed to have possessed a copy and translated it. This book, according to the *mythos*, contains the formulae for evoking incredible things into visible appearance, beings and monsters which dwell in the Abyss, and Outer Space, of the human psyche.

Such books have existed in fact, and do exist. Idries Shah tells us of a search he conducted for a copy of the *Book of Power* by the Arab magician Abdul-Kadir (see: *The Secret Lore of Magic* by Shah), of which only one copy was ever found. The *Keys* of Solomon had a similar reputation, as did *The Magus* by Barrett, until all of these works were eventually reprinted in the last fifteen years or so. The Golden Dawn, a famous British and American Occult lodge of the turn of the Century, was said to have possessed a manuscript called "the Veils of Negative Existence" by another Arab.

These were the sorcerer's handbooks, and generally not meant as textbooks or encyclopedias of ceremonial magick. In other words, the sorcerer or magician is supposed to be in possession of the requisite knowledge and training with which to carry out a complex magickal ritual, just as a cook is expected to be able to master the scrambling of eggs before he conjures an "eggs Benedict"; the grimoires, or Black Books, were simply variations on a theme, like cookbooks, different records of what previous magicians had done, the spirits they had contacted, and the successes they had. The magicians who now read these works are expected to be able to select the wheat from the chaff, in much the same fashion as an alchemist discerning the deliberate errors in a treatise on his subject.

Therefore it was (and is) insanity for the tyro to pick up a work on ceremonial Magick like the *Lesser Key of Solomon* to practice conjurations. It would also be folly to pick up Crowley's *Magick in Theory and Practice* with the same intention. Both books are definitely *not* for beginners, a point which cannot be made too often. Unfortunately, perhaps, the dread NECRONOMICON falls into this category.

Crowley's *Magick* was a testimony of what he had found in his researches into the forbidden, and forgotten, lore of past civilizations and ancient times. His *Book of the Law* was written in Cairo in the Spring of 1904, when he believed himself to be in contact with a praeter-human intelligence called Aiwass who dictated to him the Three Chapters that make up the *Book*. It had influenced him more than any other, and the remainder of his life was spent trying to understand it fully, and to make its message known to the world. It, too, contains the formulae necessary to summon the invisible into visibility, and the secrets of transformation are hidden within its pages, but this is Crowley's own NECRONOMICON, received in the Middle East in the shadow of the Great Pyramid of Gizeh, and therein is writ not only the beauty, but the Beast that yet awaits mankind.

It would be vain to attempt to deliver a synopsis of Crowley's philosophy, save that its 'leitmotif' is the Rabelaisian

Do what thou wilt shall be the whole of the Law.

The actual meaning of this phrase has taken volumes to explain, but roughly it concerns the uniting of the conscious self with the unconscious Self, a process of individuation which culminates in a rite called "Knowledge and Conversation of the Holy Guardian Angel"; the Angel signifying the pure, evolved Self.

Yet, there are many terrors on the Way to the Self, and an Abyss to cross before victory can be declared. Demons, vampires, psychic leeches, ghastly forms accost the aspiring magician from every angle, from every quarter around the circumference of the magick circle, and they must be destroyed lest they devour the magician himself. When Crowley professed to have passed the obstacles, and crossed the Abyss of Knowledge, and found his true Self, he found it was identical with the Beast of the Book of Revelation, 666, whom Christianity considers to represent the Devil. Indeed, Crowley had nothing but admiration for the Shaitan (Satan) of the so-called "devil-worshipping" cult of the Yezidis of Mesopotamia, knowledge of which led him to declare the lines that open this Introduction. For he saw that the Yezidis possess a Great Secret and a Great Tradition that extends far back into time, beyond the origin of the Sun cults of Osiris, Mithra and Christ; even before the formation of the Judaic religion, and the Hebrew tongue. Crowley harkened back to a time before the Moon was worshipped, to the "Shadow Out of Time"; and in this, whether he realized it as such or not, he had heard the "Call of Cthulhu".

Sumeria

That a reclusive author of short stories who lived in a quiet neighborhood in New England, and the manic, infamous Master Magician who called the world his home, should have somehow met in the sandy wastes of some forgotten civilization seems incredible. That they should both have become Prophets and Forerunners of a New Aeon of Man's history is equally, if not more, unbelievable. Yet, with H.P. Lovecraft and Aleister Crowley, the unbelievable was a commonplace of life. These two men, both acclaimed as geniuses by their followers and admirers, and who never actually met, stretched their legs across the world, and in the Seven League Boots of the mind they *did* meet, and on common soil . . . . Sumeria.

Sumeria is the name given to a once flourishing

civilization that existed in what is now known as Iraq, in the area called by the Greeks "Mesopotamia" and by the Arabs as, simply, "The Island" for it existed between two rivers, the Tigris and the Euphrates, which run down from the mountains to the Persian Gulf. This is the site of the fabled city of Babylon, as well as of Ur of the Chaldees and Kish, with Nineveh far to the north. Each of the seven principal cities of Sumeria was ruled by a different deity, who was worshipped in the strange, non-Semitic language of the Sumerians; a language which has been closely allied to that of the Aryan race, having in fact many words identical to that of Sanskrit (and, it is said, to Chinese!).

For no one knows where the Sumerians came from, and they vanished just as mysteriously as they appeared, after the Assyrian invasions which decimated their culture, yet providing the Assyrians with much of their mythology and religion; so much so that Sumerian became the official language of the state church, much as Latin is today of the Roman Catholic Church. They had a list of their kings *before the Flood*, which event they carefully chronicled, as did many another ancient civilization around the world. It is believed that they had a sophisticated system of astronomy (and astrology) as well as an equally sophisticated religious *rituale*. Magick, as well as history, begins at Sumer for the Western World, for it is here, in the sand-buried cuneiform tablets that recorded an Age, that the first Creation Epic is found, the first exorcism, the first ritual invocations of planetary deities, the first dark summonings of evil Powers, and, ironically, the first "burnings" of people the anthropologists call "Witches".

Lovecraft's *mythos* deals with what are known as *chthonic* dieties, that is, underworld gods and goddesses, much like the Leviathan of the Old Testament. The pronounciation of *chthonic* is 'katonic', which explains Lovecraft's famous Miskatonic River and Miskatonic University, not to mention the chief diety of his pantheon, *Cthulhu*, a sea monster who lies, "not dead, but dreaming" below the world; an Ancient One and supposed enemy of Mankind and the intelligent Race.

Cthulhu is accompanied by an assortment of other grotesqueries, such as *Azathot* and *Shub Niggurath*. It is of extreme importance to occult scholars that many of these deities had actual counterparts, at least in name, to deities of the Sumerian Tradition, that same Tradition that the Magus Aleister Crowley deemed it so necessary to "rediscover".

The Underworld in ancient Sumer was known by many names, among them *ABSU* or "Abyss", sometimes as *Nar Mattaru*, the great Underworld Ocean, and also as *Cutha* or *KUTU* as it is called in the *Enuma Elish* (the Creation Epic of the Sumerians). The phonetic similarity between Cutha and KUTU and Chthonic, as well as Cthulhu, is striking. Judging by a Sumerian grammar at hand, the word *KUTULU* or Cuthalu (Lovecraft's Cthulhu Sumerianized) would mean "The Man of KUTU (Cutha); the Man of the Underworld; Satan or Shaitan, as he is known to the Yezidis (whom Crowley considered to be the remnants of the Sumerian Tradition). The list of similarities, both between Lovecraft's creations and the Sumerian gods, as well as between Lovecraft's mythos and Crowley's magick, can go on nearly indefinitely, and in depth, for which there is no space here at the present. An exhaustive examination of Crowley's occultism in light of recent findings concerning Sumeria, and exegesis on Lovecraft's stories, is presently in preparation and is hoped to be available shortly. Until that time, a few examples should suffice.

Although a list is appended hereto containing various entities and concepts of Lovecraft, Crowley, and Sumeria cross-referenced, it will do to show how the Editor found the relationships to be valid and even startling. AZATOT is frequently mentioned in the grim pages of the *Cthulhu Mythos*, and appears in the NECRONOMICON as AZAG-THOTH, a combination of two words, the first Sumerian and the second Coptic, which gives us a clue as to Its identity. AZAG in Sumerian means "Enchanter" or "Magician"; THOTH in Coptic is the name given to the Egyptian God of Magick and Wisdom, TAHUTI, who was evoked by both the Golden Dawn and by Crowley himself (and known to the Greeks as

HERMES, from whence we get "Hermetic"). AZAG-THOTH is, therefore, a Lord of Magicians, but of the "Black" magicians, or the sorcerers of the "Other Side".

There is a seeming reference to SHUB NIGGURATH in the NECRONOMICON, in the name of a Sumerian deity, the "Answerer of Prayers", called ISHNIGARRAB. The word "Shub" is to be found in the Sumerian language in reference to the Rite of Exorcism, one of which is called *Nam Shub* and means "the Throwing". It is, however, as yet unclear as to what the combination SHUB ISHNIGARRAB (SHUB NIGGURATH) might actually mean.

There was a battle between the forces of "light" and "darkness" (so-called) that took place long before man was created, before even the cosmos as we know it existed. It is described fully in the *Enuma Elish* and in the bastardized version found in the NECRONOMICON, and involved the Ancient Ones, led by the Serpent MUMMU-TIAMAT and her male counterpart ABSU, against the ELDER GODS (called such in the N.) led by the Warrior MARDUK, son of the Sea God ENKI, Lord of Magicians of *this* Side, or what could be called "White Magicians"—although close examination of the myths of ancient times makes one pause before attempting to judge which of the two warring factions was "good" or "evil". MARDUK won this battle—in much the same way that later St. George and St. Michael would defeat the Serpent again—the cosmos was created from the body of the slain Serpent, and man was created from the blood of the slain commander of the Ancient Army, KINGU, thereby making man a descendent of the Blood of the Enemy, as well as the "breath" of the Elder Gods; a close parallel to the "sons of God and daughters of men" reference in the Old Testament. Yet, though the identity of the Victor is clear, there were—and are—certain persons and organizations that dared side with the vanquished, believing the Ancient Ones to be a source of tremendous, and most unbelievable, power.

"Let them curse it that curse the day, who are skilful to rouse Leviathan."

JOB 3:8

S.H. Hooke, in his excellent *Middle Eastern Mythology,* tells us that the Leviathan mentioned in JOB, and elsewhere in the Old Testament, is the Hebrew name given to the Serpent TIAMAT, and reveals that there was in existence either a cult, or scattered individuals, who worshipped or called up the Serpent of the Sea, or Abyss. Indeed, the Hebrew word for Abyss that is found in GENESIS 1:2 is, Hooke tells us, *tehom*, which the majority of scholars take to be a survival of the name of the chaos-dragon TIAMAT in the Hebrew text. It is this TIAMAT or Leviathan that is identified closely with KUTULU or Cthulhu within the pages of the NECRONOMI-CON, although both names are mentioned independently of each other, indicating that somehow KUTULU is the male counterpart of TIAMAT, similar to ABSU.

This monster is well known to cult worship all over the world. In China, however, there is an interesting twist. Far from being considered a completely hostile creature, dedicated to the erasure of mankind from the page of existence, the Dragon is given a place of pre-eminence and one does not hear of a Chinese angel or saint striving to slay the dragon, but rather to cultivate it. The Chinese system of geomancy, *feng shui* (pronounced *fung shway*) is the science of understanding the "dragon currents" which exist beneath the earth, these same telluric energies that are distilled in such places as Chartres Cathedral in France, Glastonbury Tor in England, and the Ziggurats of Mesopotamia. In both the European and Chinese cultures, the Dragon or Serpent is said to reside somewhere "below the earth"; it is a powerful force, a magickal force, which is identified with mastery over the created world; it is also a power that can be summoned by the few and not the many. However, in China, there did not seem to be a backlash of fear or resentment against this force as was known in Europe and Palestine, and the symbol of might and kingship in China is still the Dragon. In the West, the conjuration, cultivation, or worship of this Power was strenuously opposed with the advent of the Solar, Monotheistic religions and those who clung to the Old Ways were effectively extinguished. The wholesale slaughter of those called "Witches" during the Inquisition is an example of this, as well as the solemn and twisted—that is to say, purposeless and unenlightened—celibacy that the Church espoused. For the *orgone* of Wilhelm Reich is just as much Leviathan as the Kundalini of the Tantrick adepts, and the Power raised by the Witches. It has *always*, at least in the past two thousand years, been associated with occultism and essentially with Rites of Evil Magick, or the Forbidden Magick, of the Enemy, and of Satan . . .

. . . and the twisting, sacred Spiral formed by the Serpent of the Caduceus, and by the spinning of the galaxies, is also the same Leviathan as the Spiral of the biologists' Code of Life: DNA

The Goddess of the Witches

The current revival of the cult called WICCA is a manifestation of the ancient secret societies that sought to tap this telluric, occult force and use it to their own advantage, and to the advantage of humanity, as was the original intent. The raising of the Cone of Power through circle dancing is probably the simplest method of attaining results in "rousing Leviathan", and has been used by societies as diverse as the Dervishes in the Middle East and the Python Dancers of Africa, not to mention the round dances that were familiar to the Gnostic Christians, and the ones held every year in the past at Chartres.

The Witches of today, however, while acknowledging the importance of the Male element of telluric Power, generally prefer to give the greater honor to the Female Principle, personified as the Goddess. The Goddess has also been worshipped all over the world, and under many names, but is still essentially the same Goddess. That TIAMAT was undoubtedly female is to the point; and that the Chinese as well as the Sumerians perceived of *two* dragon currents, male and female, gives the researchers a more complex picture. The Green Dragon and the Red Dragon of the alchemists are thus identified, as the positive and negative energies that comprise the cosmos of our perception, as manifest in the famous Chinese *yin-yang* symbol.

But what of INANNA, the single planetary diety having a *female* manifestation among the Sumerians? She is invoked in the NECRONOMICON and identified as the vanquisher of Death, for she descended into the Underworld and defeated her *sister*, the Goddess of the Abyss, Queen ERESHKIGAL (possibly another name for TIAMAT). Interestingly enough, the myth has many parallels with the Christian concept of Christ's death and resurrection, among which the Crucifixion (INANNA was impaled on a stake as a corpse), the three days in the Sumerian Hades, and the eventual Resurrection are outstanding examples of how Sumerian mythology previewed the Christian religion by perhaps as many as *three thousand years*—a fact that beautifully illustrates the cosmic and eternal nature of this myth.

Therefore, the Goddess of the Witches has two distinct forms: the Ancient One, Goddess of the Dragon-like telluric Power which is raised in Magickal rituals, and the Elder Goddess, Defeater of Death, who brings the promise of Resurrection and Rejuvenation to her followers those who must reside for a time after death and between incarnations in what is called the "Summerland".

Sumer-land?

Another hallmark of the Craft of the Wise is evident within the NECRONOMICON, as well as in general Sumerian literature, and that is the arrangement of the cross-quarter days, which make up half of the Craft's official pagan holidays. These occur on the eves of February 2nd, May 1st, August 1st, and November 1st, and are called Candlemas, Beltane, Lammas and Samhain (or Hallows), respectively.

The name Lammas has a curious origin in the dunes at Sumer. It is no less than the name of one of the four mythological Beasts of the astrological fixed signs, Lamas being the name of the half-lion, half-man Guardian of Leo (the sign governing most of August, when the feast of Lammas takes place), and USTUR being that of Aquarius (February), SED that of Taurus (May) and NATTIG that of Scorpio (November). I do not believe that this is a fantastic assumption, the Sumerian origin of the Feast of Lammas. Indeed, it seems just as valid as the ideas of Idries Shah concerning Craft etymology as presented in his book, *The Sufis.* It is also not far-fetched to assume that these four beasts were known to the entire region of the Middle East, as they appear on the Sphinx in Egypt, and have become the symbols of the Four Evangelists of the Christian New Testament—an ironic and splendid result of the ignorance of the Greek religious historians concerning the ancient mysteries!

Probably the most inconsistent concept the Sumerians possessed with reference to the Craft is the naming of the Goddess as a deity, not of the Moon (as the Craft would have it), but of the planet Venus. The Moon was governed by a *male* divinity, NANNA (like INANNA but minus the initial 'I'), and was considered the Father of the Gods by the earliest Sumerian religion. It should be noted, however, that all of the planetary deities, termed "the zoned Ones" or *zonei* in Greek, and indeed all of the Sumerian deities, had both male and female manifestations, showing that the Sumerians definitely recognized a yin-yang composition of the universe (the "male Moon" idea is, the Editor is given to understand, common to the so-called Aryan mythologies). There is also evidence to show that every god and goddess also had both a good and an evil nature, and evil gods were banished in the exorcism formulae of that civilization as well as the lesser forms of demon.

The Horned Moon

As mentioned, the God of the Moon was called NANNA by the Sumerians. By the later Sumerians and Assyrians, he was called SIN. In both cases, he was the Father of the Gods (of the planetary realm, the *zonei*), and was depicted as wearing horns, a symbol familiar to the Witches as representative of their God. The horn shaped crown is illustrative of the crescent phases of the Moon, and were symbolic of divinity in many cultures around the world, and were also thought to represent certain animals who were horned, and worshipped for their particular qualities, such as the goat and bull. They also represent sexual power.

The fact that, in ancient Sumeria and Egypt, horns were not solely representative of evil gods, but of many different deities, was used by the Christian Church in their attempt to eradicate the pagan faiths. It was a simple enough symbol to identify with the Author of Evil, Satan, which the Church depicted as a half-animal, half-human creature with horns, claws, and sometimes a tail. The Church's use of the horns as a sort of archetype of Evil is quite similar to the feeling many people have today with regards to the swastika used by the Nazis, a symbol which has become the archetype of an evil sigil in the West. The fact that it is a highly valued mystical and religious symbol in the East is something that is not well-known. What is worse, the image of the Devil as perpetrated by the Church is simultaneously representative of sexual energy, and can be safely compared to Jung's archetype of the Shadow, the psychic repository of a man's innate *maleness*, as the *anima* represents that part of a man which is feminine. Truly, the pictures painted of a Satanic ritual by the pious Catholic clergymen was one of sexual orgies and "perversions", and the handbook of the Inquisitors, the *Malleus Maleficarum*—which has been responsible for the deaths of many more people than even Hitler's *Mein Kampf*—is full of detailed sexual imagery and reveals the nature of the souls of the monks who wrote it, rather than of the innocents it was used to massacre. Eventually, Satanism, Protestantism and Judaism were inextricably woven together to form a patchwork quilt of Evil that the Church attempted to destroy during the Middle Ages, with fire and sword.

As a matter of fact, a certain type of devil worship did exist during those times but, ironically, the acolytes of Hell were usually never brought to trial; something which stems from the fact that many of those who celebrated and attended the infamous Black Masses of the period were Roman Catholic clergymen, many of whom has been pressed into His Service at a young age by their parents, who wished to see their sons brought up well-fed and educated in those uncertain times, where the Church was the sole power and refuge. The frustration at being "condemned" to a life that demanded the abandonment of society and a "normal" life led many priests to express their hostilities through the Office of the Demon, the Black Mass. Often, this was also a means of *political* demonstration, as the Church controlled virtually all the political life of the period. In a way, as though in a test tube at a philosophical laboratory, Aleister Crowley was brought up under similar circumstances—although very far removed in time from the days of the Church's immense temporal power. Coming from a fanatically religious Christian family, and suddenly freed upon the neighborhood of Cambridge, Crowley did, in a sense, turn Satanist. He identified strongly with the underdog, politically as well as spiritually, and came eventually to take the Name of the Beast as his own, and expound a philosophy that he hoped would rip apart the worn tapestry of the established moral Christian atmosphere of Victorian

England, and expose it for what it really was, a carpet made of many ingenious threads and not God—or eternal happiness—at all; only nap.

Therefore, it seemed almost logical that he should seek in the defeated, Old Religions of the world for the basis of his new philosophy and, some say, his new "religion". He raised the female aspect back up to one of equality with the male, as it was in the rites of Egypt, and of Eleusis. "Our Lady Babalon" (his spelling) became a theme of many of his magickal writings, and he received his Credo, the *Book of the Law*, through a Woman, his wife Rose Kelly. The lunar element, as well as the Venusian, are certainly accessible in his works. It has even been said in occult circles that he had a hand in putting together the grimoire of one Gerald Gardner, founder of a contemporary Witchcraft movement, called the *Book of Shadows*.

The Moon has an extremely important, indeed indispensable, role in the tantrick sex magick rites that so pre-occupied Crowley and the O.T.O. There can be no true magick without woman, nor without man, and in the symbolic language of the occult there can be no Sun without the Moon. In alchemy, ceremonial magick, and Witchcraft, the formula is the same, for they all deal with identical properties; whether they are called the Sun and Moon of the Elixir Vitae, the male and female participants in a rite of Indian or Chinese tantricism, or the Shadow and Anima of Jungian depth psychology.

For many years, the Moon remained the prime diety of the Sumerians, constituting the essential Personum of a religious and mystical drama that was performed roughly 3000 B.C. amid the deserts and marshes of Mesopotamia. Side by side with the worship of the Moon, NANNA, there was fear of the Demon, PAZUZU; a genie so amply recreated in the book and the movie by Blatty, *The Exorcist*, and similarly recognized as the Devil Himself by the Church. PAZUZU, the Beast, was brought to life by Aleister Crowley, and the Demon walked the Earth once more.

With publicity provided by H.P. Lovecraft.

PAZUZU was a prime example of the type of Devil of which the Sumerians were particularly aware, and which they depicted constantly in their carvings and statues. The purpose of this iconography was to ward off the spiritual—and psychic—circumstances which would precipitate a plague, or some other evil. "Evil to destroy evil." Although the ancient peoples of the world were conscious of an entity we might call the "Author of all Evil", the Devil or Satan, as evident in the Sumerian Creation Epic and the rumored existence of the Cult of Set of the Egyptians, the more pressing concern was usually the exorcism of the "little devils" that tormented society. There is no exorcism of TIAMAT, she exists, somehow, just as the Abyss exists and is perhaps indispensable to human life if we think of Her as typifying the female quality of Energy. Although MARDUK was responsible for halving the Monster from the Sea, the Sumerian Tradition has it that the Monster is not dead, but dreaming, asleep below the surface of the Earth, strong, potent, dangerous, and very real, Her powers can be tapped by the knowledgeable, "who are skillful to rouse Leviathan."

Although the Christian religion has gone to great lengths to prove that the Devil is inferior to God and exists solely for His purpose, as the Tempter of Man—surely a dubious *raison d'etre*—the Sumerian Tradition acknowledges that the Person of "Evil" is actually the oldest, most Ancient of the Gods. Whereas Christianity states that Lucifer was a rebel in heaven, and fell from God's grace to ignominy below, the original story was that MARDUK was the rebel, and severed the Body of the Ancient of Ancient Ones to create the Cosmos, in other words, the precise reverse of the Judeo-Christian dogma. The Elder Gods evidently possessed a certain Wisdom that was not held by their Parents, yet their Parents held the Power, the Primal Strength, the First Magick, that the Elder Ones tapped to their own advantage, for they were begotten of Her.

It is generally accepted in the Halls of Magick that all of the Wisdom in the world is useless without the necessary adjunct of Power. This Power has gone by many names, as the Goddess and the Devil have, but the Chinese symbolize It by the Dragon. It is the force of Will, and relies heavily upon the biochemical matter that makes up the human body and, hence, the human consciousness, to give it existence. Science is coming around to accept the fact that the Will does exist, just at the point where Psychology has determined it does not—in the behaviorist's vain attempt to eradicate what has always been known to constitute vital parts of the psyche from their consideration in pseudo scientific experimentation, leaving us with the "white mice and pigeons" of Koestler's *The Ghost In The Machine*. Science, ancient Sister of Magick, has begun to realize the human potential that resides, inconspicuously, in the spiral-mapped matter of the brain. Just as the magicians, accused of trafficking with the Devil, were said to have developed tremendous power over natural phenomena, Science has ascended to that realm unblamed, and guiltless. The Pope has ridden in aircraft. Cardinals have flown in 'choppers' over battlefields in Southeast Asia, urging technological eco-cide, invoking Christ; pronouncing damnation and the Devil on the industrially inferior man. *Ecce Qui Tollit Peccata Mundi.*

And a rock group from England, home of the Anglican heresy, sings of "sympathy" for the Devil. PAZUZU. TIAMAT. The Seven Deadly Sins. The fear of Lovecraft. The pride of Crowley.

The lunar landing was the symbolic manifestation of man's newly acquired potential power to alter the nature—and, perhaps, via nuclear weapons, the course—of the heavenly bodies, the *zonei*, the Elder Gods. It is a power the Ancient Ones have been waiting for, for millenia, and it is now within their grasp. The next century may deliver unto mankind this awesome power and responsibility, and will leave him knocking on the dread doors of the *azonei*, the IGIGI, approaching the barrier that keeps out the ABSU.

And one day, without benefit of NECRONOMI-CON, the Race of Man will smash the barrier and the Ancient

Ones will rule once more.

An alternative possibility exists: that, by landing on the Moon, we have come to reinstate the ancient Covenant and thereby assure our protection against the Outside. Since "the gods are forgetful", by treading on their celestial spheres we are reminding them of their ancient obligations to us, their created ones. For, as it is said in one of man's most ancient of Covenants, the Emerald Table, "As Above, So Below". Man's power to alter the nature of his environment must develop simultaneously with his ability to master his *inner* environment, his own mind; his psyche, soul, spirit. Perhaps, then, the lunar landing was the first collective initiation for humanity, which will bring it one step closer to a beneficent Force that resides beyond the race of the "cruel celestial spirits", past the Abyss of Knowledge. Yet, he must remember that the occult powers that accompany magickal attainment are ornamental only, indications of obstacles overcome on the Path to Perfection, and are not to be sought after in themselves, for therein lies the truth Death. Lovecraft saw this Evil, as the world passed from one War and moved menacingly toward another. Crowley prepared for it, and provided us with the formulae. The Mad Arab saw it all, in a vision, and wrote it down. He was, perhaps, one of the most advanced adepts of his time, and he certainly has something to say to us, today, in a language the Intuition understands. Yet they called him "Mad".

Accompanied in the ranks of the "insane" by such "madmen" as Neitzsche, Artaud, and Reich, the Mad Arab makes a Fourth, in a life-and-death game of cosmic Bridge. They are all voices crying in that wilderness of madness that men call Society, and as such were ostracized, stoned, and deemed mentally unfit for life. But, for them, Justice will come when we have realized that the Ship of State and the Ship of St. Peter have become mere Ships of Fools—with Captains who course the seas by stars, ignoring the eternal Ocean—and then, we will have to look to the Prisoners in the Hold for navigational guidance.

It is there, always, and Cthulhu Calls.

PREFATORY NOTES

THE PRESENT MANUSCRIPT was delivered into the hands of the Editor by a priest who had managed to get ordained through uncanonical methods which have been entertainingly described in the several books and articles on tht ecclesiastic phenomenon, the "wandering bishops". Just such an "unorthodox" prelate was Fr. Montague Summers, who wrote numerous books on demonology, witchcraft, and the like. Suffice it to say, we were rather doubtful as to the authenticity of the work before us. In the first place, it was in Greek and for quite awhile it was difficult to ascertain what it might actually be, save for the title NECRONOMICON and the many weird drawings. In the second place, after translation, we found several internal inconsistencies and some evidence that would suggest we did not possess the entire Work. There may still be some missing or the irregular monastic might have withheld certain of the chapters. As the chapters are not numbered, it is too difficult to say.

A great deal of misfortune accompanied the publication of this book. First, we went through more than one translator. The last finally absconded with his preface, describing his work in some detail. This, we will have to do from memory in the following pages. At one point, an unscrupulous publisher from the West Coast took a copy of the initial preface and some of the miscellaneous pages in translation (including some dummies, which we were in the habit of giving potential publishers for our protection) and went off, and has not been heard from again.

At a crucial stage in the preparation of the manuscript, the Editor was stricken with a collapsed lung and had to undergo emergency surgery to save his life.

But, let us proceed with a description of the contents of the NECRONOMICON:

Within these pages a series of myths and rituals are presented that have survived the darkest days of magick and occultism. The exorcisms and bindings of the famous *Maqlu* text are here presented for the first time in English, although not completely: for the originals in their entirety were evidently not known to the author of the NECRONOMICON, nor are they to present scholarship; the various tablets upon which they were written being cracked and effaced in many places, rendering translation impossible. The MAGAN text, which comprises the Creation Epic of the Sumerians (with much later glosses) and the account of Inanna's "descent into the Underworld", along with more extraneous matter, is presented. The unique "Book of the Entrance" has no counterpart in occult literature, and the drawings of magickal seals and symbols are wholly new to anything that has yet appeared on the contemporary occult scene—although bearing some resemblances to various diagrams found in the ancient Arabic texts of the last millenium. Although some of the characters found in these pages can be traced to Mandaic and Demotic sources, and are evidently of a much later date than the Rites of Sumer, the overall appearance of the seals is quite unusual, almost surreal.

The Book begins with an introduction by the alleged author, the Mad Arab (the name that Lovecraft made famous, 'Abdul Alhazred' does not appear in our copy of the Ms.), and ends with a sort of epilogue by the same Arab. We have called the first part "The Testimony of the Mad Arab" and the latter "The Testimony of the Mad Arab, The Second Part." The Second Part is the most chilling. The author has, by this stage in the writing of his opus, become fearful for his soul and begins to repeat himself in the text, saying things he has already said in previous chapters as though having forgotten he had said them, or perhaps to stress their importance. The Second Testimony is riddled through with *non sequiturs* and bits of incantation.

He does not finish the Book.

It trails off where he would have signed it,

presumably, in the Arab manner, by giving his lineage. Instead, it ends before he can name himself or even one relation. We can only imagine with horror what fate befell this noble Sage.

Another problem that confronts the Editor is the suspected frequency of copyist's glosses; that is, there do seem to be occasionally bits of sentence or fragments of literature that would seem to be inconsistent with the period in which the text was written. However, no final word can be said on this matter. The difficulty arises in the age-old question of "which came first, the chicken or the egg?". For instance, in the MAGAN text, the final verses read as though from the Chaldean Oracles of Zoroaster:

"Stoop not down, therefore, into the darkly shining world," which might have been of Greek origin and not Zoroastrian. It is a question for scholars.

The etymology of certain words is a game that has fascinated both the Editor and perhaps a score or more of Sumerian researchers of the past. The Sumerian origin of many of the words and place-names we use today provides us with an insight into our own origins. For instance, the Sumerian word for temple is BAR, from which we get our word "barrier", or so it is said by Waddell. This makes sense in the context of the NECRONOMICON which is very much concerned with the erecting and maintaining of barriers against the hostile forces Outside.

The etymology is even dramatic where Magick is concerned, and aids us in understanding even Crowley's system better than we do. As an example, Crowley (or Aiwass) ends the *Book of the Law* with the words "AUM.HA." In the *Sumero-Aryan Dictionary* by Waddell we read that the word AUM was known to the Sumerians, in almost the same sense that it was, and is, known to the Hindus. It is a sacred word, and pertains to the Lord of Magicians, ENKI. Further, the Greek spelling of ENKI was EA, by which he is most commonly known in the European texts which treat of Sumeriology. In the Greek alphabet, EA would appear as HA.

Q.E.D.: AUM.HA betrays the essential Sumerian character of that Book.

After the initial Testimony, we come to the chapter entitled "Of The ZONEI and Their Attributes". *Zonei* is, of course, a Greek word and refers to the planetary, or heavenly, bodies; for they are "zoned", i.e., having set courses and spheres. They are also known as such in the Chaldean Oracles. The 'spirits' or bodies that exist beyond the *zonei* are called the *azonei*, meaning "un-zoned". Whether this refers to the so-called "fixed" stars (having no sphere ascertainable to the early astronomers) or to the comets, is unknown to the Editor. Whatever the case may be, the *zonei* seem to include the Seven Philosophical Planets, i.e., including the Sun and Moon as planetary bodies, along with Mercury, Venus, Mars, Jupiter and Saturn. Each has their own seal and their own Number.

Kenneth Grant, author of *Aleister Crowley and the Hidden God*, may be interested to know (or may already know) that the Number of the Sumerian Goddess of Venus, hence of Love and War, is Fifteen. In many of the ancient tablets of that period, she is actually referred to as "the Fifteen", as a shortcut to spelling out the whole Name in cuneiform, we assume. Grant made much of "the Goddess Fifteen" in his study of Crowley's system as related to Tantricism, without mentioning the Name by which this Goddess is quite well-known, or even mentioning Her native country!

After the chapter on *Zonei*, we come to the "Book of Entrance" which is really a system of self-initiation into the planetary spheres and may have something to do with the planetary arrangement of the steps of the ziggurats of Mesopotamia, which were seven-storeyed mountains. Not much is revealed to the potential candidate for initiation as to how these "gates" work, or what he might find there, save to say that the key of one Gate lies in mastering the Gate before it. The Mad Arab was either keeping a sacred Secret, or found human language inadequate to the task of describing what other initiates in similar systems have expressed in the vague abstractions of the truly illuminated, likening the experience to an LSD trip.

The "Incantations of the Gates" follow, and are probably meant to accompany the preceding chapter, being prayers proper to each of the celestial Gates. The "Conjuration of the Fire God" follows this, and resembles the others in its mixture of Greek and Sumerian phrases. It should be noted here that wherever a Sumerian phrase appears in the original MS. we have kept it as it is, untranslated, as we expect the Mad Arab would have wanted it. Quite possibly, even he did not know the exact meanings of much of the conjurations in the Old Tongue, but viewed it as a 'barbarous tongue' which must be preserved because of its essential Power. Indeed, with the publication of this Book, Sumerian may become as popular among magicians as the strange, angelic language of Enochian, discovered by Dr. Dee in Elizabethan England.

In Greek, in the original MS., a common incantation would look something like this (using Roman characters for the Greek):

> 'O Kakos Theos
> 'O Kakos Daimon
> 'O Daimon
> PNEUMA TOU OURANOU
>   THUMETHETE!
> PNEUMA TES GES THUMETHATE!
> (O Wicked God
> O Wicked Demon
> O Demon
> Spirit of the Sky, Remember!
> Spirit of the Earth, Remember!)

Yet, a word like SHAMMASH, the Name of the Solar Diety, would read SAMAS or SAMMAS, and in the text of the NECRONOMICON we would use the correct transliteration (phonetic) which would make the word read like its original.

The "Conjuration of the Watcher" follows the Fire God conjuration. The word "watcher" is sometimes used synonymously with "angel", and sometimes as a distinct Race, apart from *angelos: egregori*. The Race of Watchers are said not to care what they Watch, save that they follow orders. They are somewhat mindless creatures, but quite effective. Perhaps they correspond to Lovecraft's *shuggoths*, save that the latter became unweildly and difficult to manage.

After the Watcher, comes the MAKLU text, which appears to be a collection of exorcisms, which includes the famous "Xilka Xilka Besa Besa" incantation, in the original, to which a translation has been appended in this work—a translation evidently not at hand when the author compiled the MS. Thus, for the first time, this much-rumored exorcism is available in full and in English.

After this, the "Book of Calling" needs little explanation. It is the grimoire of the NECRONOMICON, containing the formulae of ritual conjuration, as well as the seals and diagrams to accompany the rites. It is followed by "The Book of Fifty Names" being fifty separate powers of the God MARDUK, defeater of Chaos. This is interesting, in that the names seem to come from the *Enuma Elish*, in which the Elder Gods confer these fifty names upon Marduk as titles, in their appreciation of his routing of Evil. A sigil is given for each of the Names, and a word of Power for most of them.

Then appears the Centerpiece of the Book, the MAGAN text. The word MAGAN may mean the Land of the Magan which was said to lie in the West of Sumer. For a time, it seems the name Magan was synonymous with the Place of Death—as the Sun 'died' in the West. Hence, it is a bit confusing as to what Magan is really supposed to mean in this text, but in context the "Place of Death" explanation seems quite valid. The MAGAN text is nothing more than an incomplete and free-form version of the Creation Epic of Sumer, along with Inanna's Descent into the Underworld, and many glosses. We are told how MARDUK slays TIAMAT— after much the same fashion that the Chief of Police of Amity slays the great white shark in Benchley's novel JAWS, blowing an evil wind (the oxygen tank) into Her mouth and sending in an arrow (bullet) in after it to explode her. Surely, the two or three most box-office successful films of the past few years, JAWS, THE EXORCIST and, perhaps, THE GODFATHER, are an indication that the essence of Sumerian mythology is making itself felt in a very real way in this, the latter half of the Twentieth Century?

After the long and poetic MAGAN text, comes the URILLIA text which might be Lovecraft's *R'lyeh Text,* and is subtitled "Abominations". It has more specifically to do with the worship of the Serpent, and the nature of the cults that participate in the Concelebration of Sin. Again, more conjurations and seals are given, even though the reader is charged not to use them; an inconsistency that is to be found in many grimoires of any period and perhaps reveals a little of the magician's mentality; for there is very little that is evil to the advanced magus, who cares not if he deal with angelic or demonic forces, save that he gets the job done!

Then, following the URILLIA text and forming the very end of the received MS., is the Second Part of the Testimony of the Mad Arab. It is a haunting and sorrowful melody of the mind of this much talked-about but little-known occult personality. Was he really Mad? This is perhaps a question that will go on for as long as Man tries to understand himself; himself as a part of the cosmic dance and spiral, which includes the satanic as well as the deific, the sad as well as the happy. Perhaps the Arab was privvy to some other-worldly secret that he could not reveal. Perhaps he had opened the Door by mistake, his own personal Gate to the Abyss, and was forced to cross its threshold into the Unknown. We may never know.

Or, we may wish we never had.

The Editor
New York, New York
October 12, 1975

CHART OF COMPARISONS

(showing some relationships to be found between the mythos of Lovecraft, the magick of Crowley, and the faith of Sumer.)

Lovecraft	Crowley	Sumer
Cthulhu	The Great Beast as represented in "CTHΛH 666"	Ctha-lu, Kutulu
The Ancient Ones	Satan; Teitan	Tiamat
Azathoth	Aiwass (?)	Azag-thoth
The Dunwich Horror	Choronzon	Pazuzu
Shub Niggurath	Pan	Shub Ishniggarab (?)
Out of Space	The Abyss	Absu; Nar Mattaru
IA!	IO! IAO!	IA (JAH; EA; Lord of Waters)
The Five-pointed grey Star carven	The Pentagram	The AR, or UB (Plough Sign; the original pentagram and sign of the Aryan Race)
Vermis Mysteriis	The Serpent	Erim (the Enemy; and the Sea as Chaos; Gothic: Orm, or Worm, great Serpent)

This is, of course, by no means a complete list but rather an inspirational sampling. Meditation upon the various Things mentioned in the Mythos will permit the scholar to draw his own conclusions; research upon the etymology of both Lovecraft's and Crowley's respective literature enables the occultist to discover the ancient Names and Numbers for much of his own, familiar, material.

(Note: that Lovecraft may have heard of Crowley is hinted at darkly in his short story "The Thing On The Doorstep" in which he refers to a cult leader from England who had established a covenstead of sorts in New York. In that story, published in *Weird Tales* in 1936, the cult leader is closely identified with chthonic forces, is described as "notorious", and linked to the strange fate that befell the protagonist, Edward Derby.)

THE CHART that follows is based on research presently available to the Editor with regard to Sumerian and Assyro-Babylonian religions. Entries in parentheses refer to the state of Correspondences before the advent of the Elder Gods, the Race of Marduk; that is, it reflects the nature of the cosmos before the Fall of Marduk from Heaven. (Names of zodiacal constellations are after Budge's renderings.)

	Table VII [A.C.]	*Table XXV* [S.]
0.	. . .	ANU (TIAMAT)
1.	Sphere of the Primum Mobile	ENLIL (ABSU)
2.	Sphere of the Zodiac or Fixed Stars	ENKI; LUMASHI (IGIGI)
3.	Sphere of Saturn	ADAR
4.	Sphere of Jupiter	MARDUK
5.	Sphere of Mars	NERGAL
6.	Sphere of the Sun	UTU
7.	Sphere of Venus	INANNA
8.	Sphere of Mercury	NEBO
9.	Sphere of the Moon	NANNA
10.	Sphere of the Elements	KIA
11.	Air	ANNA
12.	Mercury	GUDUD
13.	Moon	SIN
14.	Venus	DLIBAT
15.	Aries	AGRU (XUBUR)
16.	Taurus	KAKKAB U ALAP SHAME (KINGU)

17. Gemini	RE'U KINU SHAME U TU'AME RABUTI (VIPER)
18. Cancer	SHITTU (SNAKE)
19. Leo	KALBU RABU (LAKHAMU)
20. Virgo	SHIRU (WHIRLWIND)
21. Jupiter	UMUNPADDU
22. Libra	ZIBANITUM (Ravening Dog)
23. Water	BADUR
24. Scorpio	AKRABU (SCORPION-MAN)
25. Sagittarius	PA-BIL-SAG (HURRICANE)
26. Capricorn	SUXUR MASH (FISH-MAN)
27. Mars	MASTABARRU
28. Aquarius	GULA (HORNED BEAST)
29. Pisces	DILGAN U RIKIS NUNI (WEAPON)
30. Sun	SHAMASH
31. Fire	AG
32. Saturn	KAIMANU
32. (bis) Earth	KIA
31. (bis) Spirit	ZI

NOTES ON PRONOUNCIATION

WE CANNOT BE absolutely certain how Sumerian and Akkadian were spoken; but many useful guidelines are available to the student, including the transliterated tablets found all over Mesopotamia. Basically, we can offer the following principles which should prove of value in reciting the foreign language instructions:

Vowels

a as in "f*a*ther"
e as in "wh*e*y"
i as in "ant*i*que"
o as in "b*o*at" (but rarely found)
u as in "z*u*lu"

Consonants

Most are basically the same as in English. The Sumerians did not have an alphabet as we know it, but they had developed a syllabry, very much like the Japanese "Kana" script of today. In phonetic transliterations, the English spelling sought to approximate the Sumerian pronunciation. However, there are a few sounds which English does not possess, and which have been put into phonetic variations. Important examples below:

X as in the German "ach"
CH (same as above)
Q as in "like"
K (same as above)
SH as in "shall"
SS as in, perhaps, "lasso"; a hissing "s" common to Arabic languages
Z as in "lots"; a hard "ts" sound, not quite as in "zoo"

Remember, in the transliterations which follow, every letter must be pronounced. There are no schwas or silent syllables in Sumerian. Hence, "KIA" is pronounced "keeya"; "KAIMANU" is pronounced "ka-ee-mah-nu" or, if spoken rapidly, the two initial vowel sounds slur into "kigh" rhyming with "high".

The incantations should be said carefully and slowly at first, to familiarize oneself with the tongue-twisting phrases. A mistake may prove fatal to the Work.

THE SPELLS (TRANSLATED)

WHERE POSSIBLE, the Editor has taken every opportunity to find the original Sumerian or Akkadian translation of a given Greek charm or conjuration. These will be given here. Also, the reader will find English translations of the Sumerian charms as they are given in the NECRONOMICON. Not all of the charms are available this way, and sometimes we have had to make do with near misses. Much of what is found here has come from the *Maklu* text, of which the only extant translation is in the German of Tallqvist ("Die Assyrische Beschworungs-serie Maqlu nach dem originalen im British Museum Herausgegeben" *Acta Societatis Scientiarum Fennicae,* Tomm. XX, No. 6, Helsingforsiae mdcccxcv). The word "maklu" or "maqlu" itself is controversial, but Tallqvist seems to think that it does, indeed, mean "burning"; especially so as the incantations to be found therein invariably entail burning something, usually a doll made in the likeness of a witch or evil sorcerer that the magician wished to dispose of. Hence, we have here probably the archetype of the Great Burning Times of the Inquisition, when people were condemned to a fiery death as Witches and Pagans. The chant "burn, witch! burn!" can be found in the *Maklu* text, in all its pristine glory. Indeed, Cthulhu Calls.

The Conjuration "The Binding of the Evil Sorcerers"

Alsi ku nushi ilani mushiti
Itti kunu alsi mushitum kallatum kuttumtum
Alsi bararitum qablitum u namaritum
Ashshu kashshaptu u kashshipanni
Eli nitum ubbiraanni
Ili-ia u Ishtari-ia ushis-su-u-eli-ia
Eli ameri-ia amru-usanaku
Imdikula salalu musha u urra
Qu-u imtana-allu-u pi-ia
Upu unti pi-ia iprusu
Me mashtiti-ia umattu-u
Eli li nubu-u xiduti si-ipdi
Izizanimma ilani rabuti shima-a dababi
Dini dina alakti limda
Epu-ush salam kashshapi-ia u kashshapti-ia
Sha epishia u mushtepishti-ia
Is mass-ssarati sha mushi lipshuru ruxisha limnuti
Pisha lu-u ZAL.LU Lishanusha Lu-u Tabtu
Sha iqbu-u amat limutti-ia kima ZAL.LU litta-tuk
Sha ipushu kishpi kima Tabti lishxarmit
qi-ishrusha pu-uttu-ru ipshetusha xulluqu
Kal amatusha malla-a sseri
Ina qibit iqbu-u ilani mushitum.

The Conjuration "XILQA XILQA BESA BESA" or "A Most
Excellent Charm Against the Hordes of Demons" etc.

Arise! Arise! Go far away! Go far away!
Be shamed! Be shamed! Flee! Flee!
Turn around, go, arise and go far away!
Your wickedness may rise to heaven like unto smoke!
Arise and leave my body!
From my body, depart in shame!
From my body flee!
Turn away from my body!
Go away from my body!
Do not return to my body!
Do no come near my body!
Do not approach my body!
Do not throng around my body!
Be commanded by Shammash the Mighty!
Be commanded by Enki, Lord of All!
Be commanded by Marduk, the Great Magician of the Gods!
Be commanded by the God of Fire, your Destroyer!
May you be held back from my body!

"Another Binding of the Sorcerers"

Ssalmani-ia ana pagri tapqida duppira
Ssalmani-ia ana pagri taxira duppira
Ssalmani-ia iti pagri tushni-illa duppira
Ssalmani ini ishdi pagri tushni-illa duppira
Ssalmani-ia qimax pagri taqbira duppira
Ssalmani-ia ana qulqullati tapqida duppira
Ssalmani-ia ina igari tapxa-a duppira
Ssalmani-ia ina askuppati Tushni-illa duppira
Ssalmani-ia ina bi'sha duri tapxa-a duppira
Ssalmani-ia ana GISHBAR tapqida duppira

"The Conjuration of the Mountains of MASHU"

May the mountain overpower you!
May the mountain hold you back!
May the mountain conquer you!
May the mountain frighten you!
May the mountain shake you to the core!
May the mountain hold you in check!
May the mountain subject you!
May the mountain cover you!
May the mighty mountain fall on you,
May you be held back from my body!

(Note: the original translator had noted the resemblance between the Greek word for Lord, *kurios*, and the Sumerian word for Mountain, *kur*, and for a type of underworld, chthonic, monster which is also called *kur* and which refers to the Leviathan of the Old Testament. Also, in this particular conjuration, the word for mountain is *shadu—shaddai*? The Old Serpent KUR is, of course, invoked every day by the Christians: Kyrie Eleison!)

COMMON SUMERIAN WORDS AND
PHRASES IN ENGLISH

Akhkharu	Vampire
Alal	Destroyer
Alla Xul	Evil God
Barra!	Begone!
Dingir Xul	Evil God
Edin Na Zu!	Go to the Desert! (a form of exorcism)
Gelal	Incubus
Gigim xul	Evil Spirit
Gidim Xul	Evil Ghost
Idimmu	Demon
Idpa	Fever
Kashshaptu	Witch
Lalartu	Phantom
Lalassu	Spectre
Lilit	Succubus
Maskim Xul	Evil Fiend (Ambusher, Lier-In-Wait)
Mulla Xul	Evil Devil
Rabishu	(same as Maskim Xul)
Telal	Wicked Demon (Warrior)
Uggae	God of Death
Uruku	Larvae
Utuk Xul	Evil Spirit
Zi Dingir Anna Kanpa!	Spirit, God of the Sky, Remember!
Zi Dingir Kia Kanpa!	Spirit, God of the Earth, Remember!

A WORD CONCERNING THE
ORIGINAL MANUSCRIPT

THE EDITOR and the Publishers anticipate that there will be a demand at first for privileged views of the original NECRONOMICON, whether out of curiosity's sake, or by nervous experimenters who will be *certain* that we did not copy a sigil correctly, etc.

Let us hasten to state at this point that the original MS. is neither the property of the Editor, nor the Publishers. We were given the right to translate and publish this work, with as much additional and explanatory material as needed, but not the right to hold the MS. up to public inspection. We regret that this is the case, but we also feel that it might be advisable, in reference to the dangerous character of the work involved. Perhaps one day a book will be written on the hazards of possessing such an original work in one's home or office, including the fearful hallucinations, physical incapacities, and emotional malaise that accompanied this work from the onset of the translation to the end of its final published form.

Therefore, as a matter of policy, we cannot honor any requests to see the NECRONOMICON in its original state.

BANISHINGS

Read this section carefully.

In the interim period between the translation and the publication of this work, the Editor, along with a circle of initiates in another discipline, undertook to experiment with the rituals and forces outlined in the NECRONOMICON. In using the material alone, or within a Western ceremonial structure (such as the Golden Dawn system) we came upon startling discoveries in both cases: *there are no effective banishings for the forces invoked in the NECRONOMICON itself!* The rituals, incantations, formulae of this Book are of ancient origin, comprising some of the oldest written magickal workings in Western occult history. The deities and demons identified within have probably not been effectively summoned in nearly six thousand years. Ordinary exorcisms and banishing formulae have thus far proved extremely inadequate: this, by experienced magicians. Hence, the following recommendations.

The religion of the ancient Sumerian peoples seems to have been lunar-oriented, a religion—or religio-magickal structure—of the night, of darkness in a sense. Invocations using solar formulae have proved thus far effective in successfully banishing NECRONOMICON demons and intelligences. For instance, the *Kaddish* prayer of the Jewish faith contains some solar elements that have proved resilient to inimical genii, and the vibration of the Lord's Prayer for Christians is also a workable method.

We suggest that individual operators utilize an equivalent solar (i.e., positive *light*) invocation from their own religion or the religion of their ancestors, should they no longer have a religion or should they have changed it in their lifetime.

For best practical purposes in the beginning—for those intent on actually using the rituals contained herein—it is advisable to take especial care in the construction of the magickal circle and of all magickal defenses. A preliminary period of purification is well in order before attempting anything in this grimoire. Persons of unstable mental condition, or unstable emotional condition, should not be allowed, under any circumstances, to observe one of these rituals in progress. That would be criminal, and perhaps even suicidal. One of our colleagues was fearfully attacked by his dog directly following a fairly simple and uncomplicated formula from this book. This is definitely not a Gilbert chemistry set.

The method of the NECRONOMICON concerns deep, primeval forces that seem to *pre-exist* the normal archetypal images of the Tarot trumps and the Golden Dawn telesmatic figures. These are forces that developed outside the Judeo-Christian mainstream, and were worshipped and summoned long before the creation of the Qabala as we know it today. Hence, the ineffectiveness of the Golden Dawn banishing procedures against them. They are not necessarily demonic or qliphotic in the sense that these terms are commonly understood in the West, they just simply represent power sources largely untapped and thus far ignored by twentieth-century, mainstream consciousness.

The results of any experimentation with this book, as well as practical suggestions concerning its rituals, are welcomed by the publishers.

BIBLIOGRAPHY & SUGGESTED READING LIST

(by no means complete, but representative. alphabetically by author)

Bernhard, Bennet and Rice. *New Handbook of the Heavens,*
    New York, 1948
Budge, E.A. *Amulets and Talismans*, New York, 1970
Crowley, A. *Book Four*, Texas, 1972
    The Book of Thoth, New York, 1969
    Liber AL vel Legis, New York, 1977
    Magick, New York (undated)
    et. al.
Cumont, F. *Oriental Religions in Roman Paganism*, New York
    1956
Dornseiff. *Das Alphabet in Mystik und Magie*, Stoicheia 7,
    Leipzig, 1925
Drower, E.S. *The Book of the Zodiac,* London 1949
Fairservis, W.A. *The Origins of Oriental Civilization*, New
    York 1959
Fossey, C. *La Magie Assyrienne*, Paris 1902
de la Fuye, A. "Le Pentagramme Pythagoricien, sa diffusion,
    son emploi dans la syllabaire cuneiforme."
    Babyloniaca, Paris 1934
Genouillac, "Les dieux de l'Elam" *Recueil de Travaux relatifs
    a la philologie et a l'archaeologie Egyptiennes et
    Assyriennes.* Paris 1904 (ed. Maspero)
Grant, K. *Aleister Crowley and the Hidden God*, New York
    1974
    The Magical Revival, New York 1973
Gray, J. *Near Eastern Mythology*, New York 1969
Griffith & Thompson. *The Leyden Papyrus*, New York 1974
Hooke, S.H. *Babylonian and Assyrian Religion*, Oklahoma
    1975
    Middle Eastern Mythology, New York 1975

King, L. *Babylonian Magic and Sorcery*, London 1896

Kramer, S.N. *History Begins At Sumer*, New York 1959
    Mythologies of the Ancient World (ed.), New York 1961
    Sumerian Mythology, Pennsylvania 1972

Laurent, *La Magie et la Divination chez les Chaldeo-Assyriennes,* Paris 1894

Lenormant, F. *Science Occult; La Magie chez les Chaldeens,* Paris 1874

Lovecraft, H.P. *Tales of the Cthulhu Mythos*, New York 1973
    At The Mountains of Madness, New York 1973
    The Dunwich Horror, New York 1963
    The Lurker at the Threshold (with August Derleth), New York 1971
    et. al.

Mason, H. *Gilgamesh* (ed.), New York 1972

Neugebauer, O. *The Exact Sciences In Antiquity*, New York 1969

Pritchard, J. *Near Eastern Texts Relating to the Old Testament*, Princeton 1958

"Sapere Aude" (pseud.) *The Chaldean Oracles of Zoroaster*, New York (undated)

Seignobos, C. *The World of Babylon*, New York 1975

Seligmann, K. *Magic, Supernaturalism, and Religion*, New York 1968

Shah, I. *Oriental Magic*, New York 1973
    The Secret Lore of Magic, New York 1972
    The Sufis, New York 1973

Tallqvist, K.L. "Die Assyrische Beschworungsserie Maqlu nach dem originalen im British Museum Herausgegeben" *Acta Societatis Scientiarum Fennicae*, Helsingfors, 1895

Thompson, R.C. *Reports of the Magicians and Astrologers of Nineveh and Babylon*, London 1900
    Semitic Magic, London 1904
    The Devils and Evil Spirits of Babylonia, London 1904

THE

NECRONOMICON

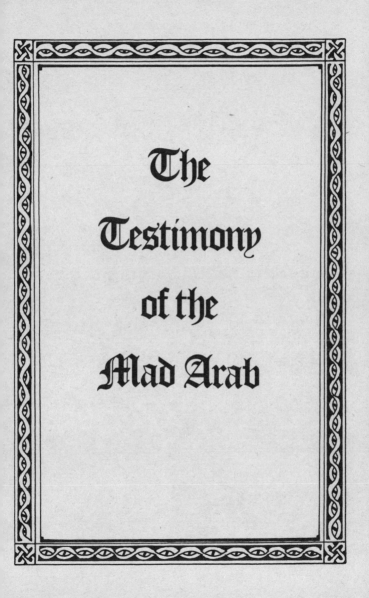

The

Testimony

of the

Mad Arab

HIS is the testimony of all that I have seen, and all that I have learned, in those years that I have possessed the Three Seals of MASSHU. I have seen One Thousand-and-One moons, and surely this is enough for the span of a man's life, though it is said the Prophets lived much longer. I am weak, and ill, and bear a great tiredness and exhaustion, and a sigh hangs in my breast like a dark lantern. I am old.

The wolves carry my name in their midnight speeches, and that quiet, subtle Voice is summoning me from afar. And a Voice much closer will shout into my ear with unholy impatience. The weight of my soul will decide its final resting place. Before that time, I must put down here all that I can concerning the horrors that stalk Without, and which lie in wait at the door of every man, for this is the ancient arcana that has been handed down of old, but which has been forgotten by all but a few men, the worshippers of the Ancient Ones (may their names be blotted out!).

And if I do not finish this task, take what is here and discover the rest, for time is short and mankind does not know nor understand the evil that awaits it, from every side, from every open Gate, from every broken barrier, from every mindless acolyte at the altars of madness.

For this is the Book of the Dead, the Book of the Black Earth, that I have writ down at the peril of my life, exactly as I received it, on the planes of the IGIGI, the cruel celestial spirits from beyond the Wanderers of the Wastes.

Let all who read this book be warned thereby that the habitation of men are seen and surveyed by that Ancient Race of gods and demons from a time before time, and that they seek revenge for that forgotten battle that took place somewhere in the Cosmos and rent the Worlds in the days before the creation of Man, when the Elder Gods walked the Spaces, the race of MARDUK, as he is known to the Chaldeans, and of ENKI our Master, the Lord of Magicians.

Know, then, that I have trod all the Zones of the Gods, and also the places of the Azonei, and have descended unto the foul places of Death and Eternal Thirst, which may be reached through the Gate of GANZIR, which was built in UR, in the days before Babylon was.

Know, too, that I have spoken with all manner of spirit and daemon, whose names are no longer known in the societies of Man, or were never known. And the seals of some of these are writ herein; yet others I must take with me when I leave you. ANU have mercy on my soul!

I have seen the Unknown Lands, that no map has ever charted. I have lived in the deserts and the wastelands, and spoken with demons and the souls of slaughtered men, and of women who have died in childbirth, victims of the she-fiend LAMMASHTA.

I have traveled beneath the Seas, in search of the Palace of Our Master, and found the stone monuments of vanquished civilizations, and deciphered the writings of some of these; while still others remain mysteries to any man who lives. And these civilizations were destroyed because of the knowledge contained in this book.

I have traveled among the stars, and trembled before the Gods. I have, at last, found the formula by which I passed the Gate ARZIR, and passed into the forbidden realms of the foul IGIGI.

I have raised demons, and the dead.

I have summoned the ghosts of my ancestors to real and visible appearance on the tops of temples built to reach the stars, and built to touch the nethermost cavities of HADES. I have wrestled with the Black Magician, AZAG-THOTH, in vain, and fled to the Earth by calling upon INANNA and her brother MARDUK, Lord of the double-headed AXE.

I have raised armies against the Lands of the East, by summoning the hordes of fiends I have made subject unto me, and so doing found NGAA, the God of the heathens, who breathes flame and roars like a thousand thunders.

I have found fear.

I have found the Gate that leads to the Outside, by which the Ancient Ones, who ever seek entrance to our world, keep eternal watch. I have smelled the vapors of that Ancient One, Queen of the Outside, whose name is writ in the terrible MAGAN text, the testament of some dead civilization whose priests, seeking power, swing open the dread, evil Gate for an hour past the time, and were consumed.

I came to possess this knowledge through circumstances quite peculiar, while still the unlettered son of a shepherd in what is called Mesopotamia by the Greeks.

When I was only a youth, traveling alone in the mountains to the East, called MASSHU by the people who live there, I came upon a grey rock carved with three strange symbols. It stood as high as a man, and as wide around as a bull. It was firmly in the ground, and I could not move it. Thinking no more of the carvings, save that they might be the work of a king to mark some ancient victory over an enemy, I built a fire at its foot to protect me from the wolves that wander in those regions and went to sleep, for it was night and I was far from my village, being Bet Durrabia. Being about three hours from dawn, in the nineteenth of Shabatu, I was awakened by the howl of a dog, or perhaps of a wolf, uncommonly loud and close at hand. The fire had died to its embers, and these red, glowing coals cast a faint, dancing shadow across the stone monument with the three carvings. I began to make haste to build another fire when, at once, the gray rock began to rise slowly into the air, as though it were a dove. I could not move or speak for the fear that seized upon my spine and wrapped cold fingers around my skull. The Dik of Azug-bel-ya was no stranger to me than this sight, though the former seemed to melt into my hands!

Presently, I heard a voice, softly, some distance away and a more practical fear, that of the possibility of robbers, took hold of me and I rolled behind some weeds, trembling. Another voice joined the first, and soon several men in the black robes of thieves came together over the place where I was, surrounding the floating rock, of which they did not exhibit the least fright.

I could see clearly now that the three carvings on the stone monument were glowing a flame red color, as though the rock were on fire. The figures were murmuring together in prayer or invocation, of which only a few words could be heard, and these in some unknown tongue; though, ANU have mercy on my soul!, these rituals are not unknown to me any longer.

The figures, whose faces I could not see or recognize, began to make wild passes in the air with knives that glinted cold and sharp in the mountain night.

From beneath the floating rock, out of the very ground where it had sat, came rising the tail of a serpent. This serpent was surely larger than any I had ever seen. The thinnest section thereof was fully that of the arms of two men, and as it rose from the earth it was followed by another, although the end of the first was not seen as it seemed to reach down into the very Pit itself. These were followed by still more, and the ground began to tremble under the pressure of so many of these enormous arms. The chanting of the priests, for I knew them now to be the servants of some hidden Power, became much louder and very nearly hysterical.

IA! IA! ZI AZAG!
IA!IA! ZI AZKAK!
IA! IA! KUTULU ZI KUR!
IA!

The ground where I was hiding became wet with some substance, being slightly downhill from the scene I was witnessing. I touched the wetness and found it to be blood. In horror, I screamed and gave my presence away to the priests. They turned toward me, and I saw with loathing that they had cut their chests with the daggers they had used to raise the stone, for some mystical purpose I could not then divine; although I know now that blood is the very food of these spirits, which is why the field after the battles of war glows with an unnatural light, the manifestations of the spirits feeding thereon.

May ANU protect us all!

My scream had the effect of casting their ritual into chaos and disorder. I raced through the mountain path by which I had come, and the priests came running after me, although some seemed to stay behind, perhaps to finish the Rites. However, as I ran wildly down the slopes in the cold night, my heart giving rise in my chest and my head growing hot, the sound of splitting rocks and thunder came from behind me and shook the very ground I ran upon. In fright, and in haste, I fell to the earth.

Rising, I turned to face whatever attacker had come nearest me, though I was unarmed. To my surprise, what I saw was no priest of ancient horror, no necromancer of that forbidden Art, but black robes fallen upon the grass and weeds, with no seeming presence of life or bodies beneath them.

I walked cautiously to the first and, picking up a long twig, lifted the robe from the tangle of weeds and thorns. All that remained of the priest was a pool of slime, like green oil, and the smell of a body lain long to rot in the sun. Such a stench nearly overpowered me, but I was resolute to find the others, to see if the same fortune had also befallen them.

Walking back up the slope that I had so fearfully run down only moments ago, I came across yet another of the dark priests, in identical condition to the first. I kept walking, passing more of the robes as I went, not venturing to overturn them any longer. Then, I finally came upon the grey stone monument that had risen unnaturally into the air at the command of the priests. It was now upon the ground once more, but the carvings still glowed with supernatural light. The serpents, or what I had then thought of as serpents, had disappeared. But in the dead embers of the fire, now cold and black, was a shining metal plate. I picked it up and saw that it also was carved, as the stone, but very intricately, after a fashion I could not understand. It did not bear the same markings as the stone, but I had the feeling I could almost read the characters, but could not, as though I once knew the tongue but had since long forgotten. My head began to ache as though a devil was pounding my skull, when a shaft of moonlight struck the metal amulet, for I know now what it was, and a voice entered into my head and told me the secrets of the scene I had witnessed in one word:

KUTULU.

In that moment, as though whispered fiercely into my ear, I understood.

These are the signs carved upon the grey stone, that was the Gate to the Outside:

And this is the amulet that I held in my hand, and hold to this very day, around my neck as I write these words:

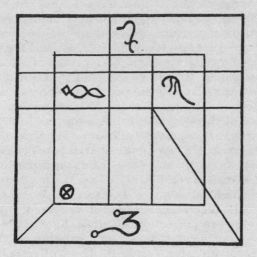

Of the three carved symbols, the first is the Sign of our Race from beyond the Stars, and is called ARRA in the tongue of the Scribe who taught it to me, an emissary of the Elder Ones. In the tongue of the eldest city of Babylon, it was UR. It is the Sigil of the Covenant of the Elder Gods, and when they see it, they who gave it to us, they will not forget us. They have sworn!

Spirit of the Skies, Remember!

The second is the Elder Sign, and is the Key whereby the Powers of the Elder Gods may be summoned, when used with the proper words and shapes. It has a Name, and is called AGGA.

The third sign is the Sigil of the Watcher. It is called BANDAR. The Watcher is a Race sent by the Elder Ones. It keeps vigil while one sleeps, provided the appropriate ritual and sacrifice has been performed: else, if called, it will turn upon you.

These seals, to be effective, must be graven on stone and set in the ground. Or, set upon the altar of offerings. Or, carried to the Rock of Invocations. Or, engraved on the metal of one's God or Goddess, and hung about the neck, but hidden from the view of the profane. Of these three, the ARRA and the AGGA may be used separately, that is to say, singly and alone. The BANDAR, however, must never be used alone, but with one or both of the others, for the Watcher must needs be reminded of the Covenant it has sworn with the Elder Gods and our Race, else it will turn upon thee and slay thee and ravage thy town until succour is to be had from the Elder Gods by the tears of thy people and the wailing of thy women.

KAKAMMU!

The metal amulet that I retrieved from the ashes of the fire, and which caught the light of the moon, is a potent seal against whatever may come in the Gate from the Outside for, seeing it, they will retreat from thee for, in the dark days of the moon, or in clouds, there can be little protection against the fiends from the Ancient Land should they break the barrier, or be let in by their servants upon the face of the earth. In such a case, no recourse is to be had until the light of the moon shines upon the earth, for the moon is the eldest among the Zonei, and is the starry symbol of our Pact. NANNA, Father of the Gods, Remember!

Wherefore, the amulet must be engraved upon pure silver in the full light of the moon, that the moon shine upon it at its working, and the essence of the moon be drawn down and captured therein. And the proper incantations must be performed, and the prescribed rituals as given forth in this Book. And the amulet must never be exposed to the light of the Sun, for SHAMMASH called UDU, in his jealousy, will rob the seal of its power. In such a case, it must be bathed in waters of camphor, and the incantations and ritual performed once again. But, verily, it were better to engrave another.

These secrets I give to thee at the pain of my life, never to be revealed to the profane, or the banished, or the worshippers of the Ancient Serpent, but to keep within thine own heart, always silent upon these things.

Peace be to thee!

Henceforth, from that fateful night in the Mountains of MASSHU, I wandered about the countryside in search of the key to the secret knowledge that had been given me. And it was a painful and lonely journey, during which time I took no wife, called no house or village my home, and dwelt in various countries, often in caves or in the deserts, learning several tongues as a traveler might learn them, to bargain with the tradespeople and learn of their news and customs. But

13

my bargaining was with the Powers that reside in each of these countries. And soon, I came to understand many things of which before I had no knowledge, except perhaps in dreams. The friends of my youth deserted me, and I them. When I was seven years gone from my family, I learned that they had all died of their own hand, for reasons no one was able to tell me; their flocks had later been slain as the victims of some strange epidemic.

I wandered as a beggar, being fed from town to town as the local people saw fit, often being stoned instead and threatened with imprisonment. On occasion, I was able to convince some learned man that I was a sincere scholar, and was thereby permitted to read the ancient records in which the details of necromancy, sorcery, magick and alchemy are given. I learned of the spells that cause men illness, the plague, blindness, insanity, and even death. I learned of the various classes of demons and evil gods that exist, and of the old legends concerning the Ancient Ones. I was thus able to arm myself against the dread Maskim, who lie in wait about the boundaries of the world, ready to trap the unwary and devour the sacrifices set out at night and in deserted places; against also the she-devil LAMMASHTA, who is called the Sword that Splits the Skull, the sight of whom causeth horror and dismay, and (some say) death of a most uncommon nature.

In time, I learned of the names and properties of all the demons, devils, fiends and monsters listed herein, in this Book of the Black Earth. I learned of the powers of the astral Gods, and how to summon their aid in times of need. I learned, too, of the frightful beings who dwell beyond the astral spirits, who guard the entrance to the Temple of the Lost, of the Ancient of Days, the Ancient of the Ancient Ones, whose Name I cannot write here.

In my solitary ceremonies in the hills, worshipping with fire and sword, with water and dagger, and with the assistance of a strange grass that grows wild in certain parts of the MASSHU, and with which I had unwittingly built my fire before the rock, that grass that gives the mind great power to travel tremendous distances into the heavens, as also into the hells, I received the formulae for the amulets and talismans which follow, which provide the Priest with safe passage among the spheres wherein he may travel in search of the Wisdom.

But now, after One Thousand-and-One moons of the journey, the Maskim nip at my heels, the Rabishu pull at my hair, Lammashta opens her dread jaws, AZAG-THOTH gloats blindly at his throne, KUTULU raises his head and stares up through the Veils of sunken Varloorni, up through the Abyss, and fixes his stare upon me; wherefore I must with haste write this Book lest my end come sooner than I had prepared. For indeed, it appears as though I have failed in some regard as to the order of the rites, or to the formulae, or to the sacrifices, for now it appears as if the entire host of ERESHKIGAL lies waiting, dreaming, drooling for my departure. I pray the Gods that I am saved, and not perish as did the Priest, ABDUL BEN-MARTU, in Jerusalem (the Gods remember and have mercy upon him!). My fate is no longer writ in the stars, for I have broken the Chaldean Covenant by seeking power over the Zonei. I have set foot on the moon, and the moon no longer has power over me. The lines of my life have been obliterated by my wanderings in the Waste, over the letters writ in the heavens by the gods. And even now I can hear the wolves howling in the mountains as they did that fateful night, and they are calling my name, and the names of the Others. I fear for my flesh, but I fear for my spirit more.

Remember, always, in every empty moment, to call upon the Gods not to forget thee, for they are forgetful and very far away. Light thy fires high in the hills, and on the tops of temples and pyramids, that they may see and remember.

Remember always to copy each of the formulae as I have put it down, and not to change it by one line or dot, not so much as a hair's breadth, lest it be rendered valueless, or worse: a broken line provides means of entrance for those Outside, for a broken star is the Gate of GANZIR, the Gate of Death, the Gate of the Shadows and the Shells. Recite the incantations as they are written here, in the manner thus prescribed. Prepare the rituals without erring, and in the proper places and times render the sacrifices.

May the Gods be ever merciful unto thee!

May thou escape the jaws of the MASKIM, and vanquish the power of the Ancient Ones!

AND THE GODS GRANT THEE DEATH BEFORE THE ANCIENT ONES RULE THE EARTH ONCE MORE!

KAKAMMU! SELAH!

Of

The Zonei

and

Their

Attributes

THE Gods of the Stars are Seven. They have Seven Seals, each of which may be used in their turn. They are approached by Seven Gates, each of which may be opened in their turn. They have Seven Colors, Seven Material Essences, and each a separate Step on the Ladder of Lights. The Chaldeans were but imperfect in their knowledge, although they had understanding of the Ladder, and certain of the formulae. They did not, however, possess the formulae for the passing of the Gates, save one, of whom it is forbidden to speak.

The passing of the Gates gives the priest both power and wisdom to use it. He becomes able to control the affairs of his life more perfectly than before, and many have been content to merely pass the first three Gates and then sit down and go no further than that, enjoying the benefits that they have found on the preliminary spheres. But this is Evil, for they are not equipped to deal with the attack from Without that must surely come, and their people will cry unto them for safety, and it will not come forth. Therefore, set thy face towards the ultimate goal and strive ever onward to the furthest reaches of the stars, though it mean thine own death; for such a death is as a sacrifice to the Gods, and pleasing, that they will not forget their people.

The ZONEI and their attributes, then, are as follows:

The God of the Moon is the God NANNA. He is
Father of the Zonei, and Eldest of the Wanderers. He is
long of beard, and bears a wand of lapis lazuli in his
palm, and possesses the secret of the tides of blood. His
color is Silver. His Essence is to be found in Silver, and
in camphor, and in those things bearing the sign of the
Moon. He is sometimes called SIN. His Gate is the first
you will pass in the rituals that follow. His Step on the
Ladder of Lights is also Silver.

This is his Seal, which you must engrave on his
metal, on the thirteenth day of the Moon in which you are
working, having no other person about you who may
watch you in its manufacture. Being finished, it should
be wrapped in a square of the finest silk and lain aside
until such time as you desire its use, and then, it should
be removed only after the Sun has gone to its rest. No ray
of sunlight should strike the Seal, lest its power be
rendered nil and a new Seal must needs be cast.

The Number of NANNA is Thirty and this is his
Seal:

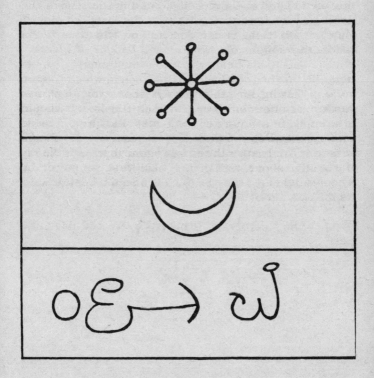

The God of Mercury is NEBO. He is a very old spirit, having a long beard, and is the guardian of the Gods, as well as the keeper of the knowledge of Science. He wears a crown of one hundred horns, and the long robe of the Priest. His color is blue. His Essence is in that metal known as Quicksilver, and is sometimes also found in sand, and in those things bearing the sign of Mercury. His Gate is the Second you will pass in the rituals that follow. His Step on the Ladder of Lights is blue.

This is his Seal, which you must write on perfect parchment, or on the broad leaf of a palm tree, having no other person about you who may watch you in its construction. Being finished, it should be wrapped in a square of the finest silk and lain aside until such time as you desire its use, and then, it should be removed only when its light is in the sky. Such is also the best time for its manufacture.

The Number of NEBO is Twelve and this is his Seal:

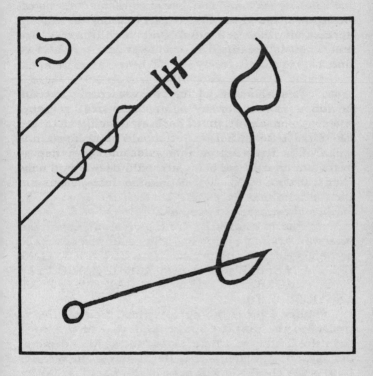

The Goddess of Venus is the most excellent Queen INANNA, called of the Babylonians ISHTAR. She is the Goddess of Passion, both of Love and of War, depending upon her sign and the time of her appearance in the heavens. She appears as a most beautiful Lady, in the company of lions, and partakes of a subtle astral nature with the Moon God NANNA. When they are in agreement, that is, when their two planets are auspiciously arranged in the heavens, it is as two offering-cups spilt freely in the heavens, to rain the sweet wine of the Gods upon the earth. And then there is great happiness and rejoicing. She sometimes appears in armor, and is thereby a most excellent guardian against the machinations of her sister, the dread Queen ERESHKIGAL of KUR. With the Name and Number of INANNA, no Priest need fear to walk into the very depths of the Underworld; for being armed, in Her armor, he is similar to the Goddess. It was thus that I descended into the foul pits that lie gaping beneath the crust of the earth, and commanded demons.

She is similarly the Goddess of Love, and bestows a favorable bride upon any man who desires it, and who makes the proper sacrifice. BUT KNOW THAT INANNA TAKES HER OWN FOR HER OWN, AND THAT ONCE CHOSEN BY HER NO MAN MAY TAKE ANOTHER BRIDE.

Her color is the purest White. Her manifestation is in the metal Copper, and also in the most beautiful flowers of a field, and in the saddest death of the battlefield, which is that field's fairest flower. Her Gate is the Third you will pass in the rites that follow, and in which place you will be of a heart to stay; but turn you face to the road that leads beyond, for that is your genuine goal, unless the Goddess choses you. Her Step on the Ladder of Lights, built of old in Babylon and at UR, is White.

This is her Seal, which you must engrave on Copper, Venus being exalted in the heavens, with no one about watching its construction. Being finished, it is to be wrapped in the purest silk and lain safely away, only to be removed when need arises, at any time.

The Number of INANNA is Fifteen, by which Number she is frequently known in the incantations of the Dispensation, her Seal is the following:

The God of the Sun is the Lord SHAMMASH, son of NANNA. He is seated upon a throne of gold, wearing a crown of two horns, holding a sceptre aloft in his right hand and a flame disk in his life, sending rays in every direction. He is the God of Light and of Life. His color is Gold. His Essence is to be found in gold, and in all golden objects and plants. He is sometimes called UDDU. His Gate is the Fourth you will pass in the rituals that follow. His Step on the great Ladder of Lights is Gold.

This is his Seal, which you must engrave in gold, when the Sun is exalted in the heavens, alone on a mountain top or some such place close to the Rays, but alone. Being finished, it should be wrapped in a square of the finest silk and lain aside until such time as it is needed.

The Number of SHAMMASH is Twenty and this is his Seal:

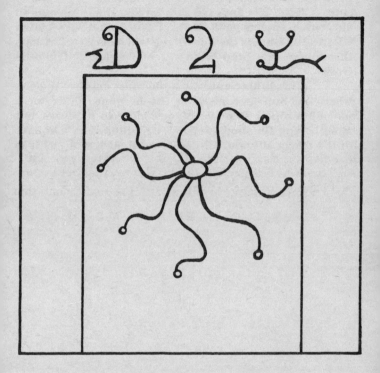

The God of Mars is the mighty NERGAL.

He has the head of a man on the body of a lion, and bears a sword and a flail. He is the God of War, and of the fortunes of War. He was sometimes thought to be an agent of the Ancient Ones, for he dwelt in CUTHA for a time. His color is dark red. His essence is to be found in Iron, and in all weapons made to spill the blood of men and of animals. His Gate is the Fifth you will see as you pass the Zones in the rituals that follow. His Step on the Ladder of Light is Red.

This is his Seal, which must be engraved on a plate of Iron, or on paper in blood, when Mars is in exaltation in the heavens. It is best done at night, far from the habitations of men and of animals, where you cannot be seen or heard. It must be wrapped first in heavy cloth, then in fine silk, and hid safe away until such times as it is needed. But to take care not to use this Seal hastily, for it is a sharp Sword.

The Number of NERGAL is Eight and this is his Seal:

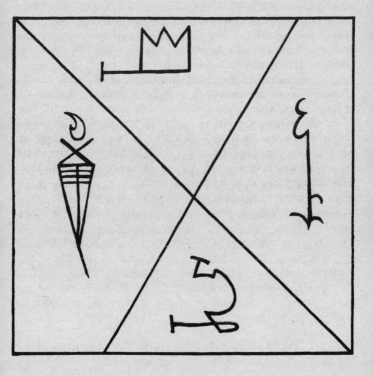

29

The God of Jupiter is the Lord of Magicians, MARDUK KURIOS of the Double-headed Axe. MARDUK was born of our Father, ENKI, to do battle against the forces of the Ancient Ones, and he won a powerful fight, subduing the armies of Evil and putting the Queen of the Ancient Ones beneath his foot. That Serpent is dead, but dreams. MARDUK was bestowed Fifty Names and Powers by the Council of the Elder Gods, which Powers he retains to this day. His color is Purple. His Essence is in the material tin, and in brass. His Gate is the Sixth that you will come upon as you follow the rituals that follow. His Step on the Ladder of Lights is Purple.

This is his Seal, which you must engrave on a plate of tin or of brass, when Jupiter is strong in the heavens, while making special invocation to ENKI Our Master. This shall be wrought as the others, and wrapped in pure silk and lain away until the time for its use. Know that MARDUK appears as a mighty warrior with a long beard and a flaming disk in his hands. He carries a bow and a quiver of arrows, and treads about the heavens keeping the Watch. Take care to summon his assistance in only the most terrible of circumstances, for his might is powerful and his anger fierce. When thou hast need of the powers of the star Jupiter, call instead one of the appropriate Powers listed within these pages, and they will surely come.

The Number of Marduk is Ten and this is his Seal:

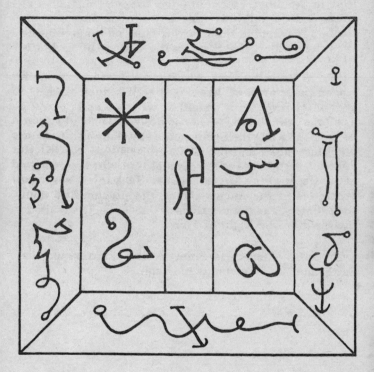

The God of Saturn is NINIB called ADAR, the Lord of Hunters and of Strength. He appears with a crown of horns and a long sword, wearing a lion's skin. He is the final Zonei before the terrible IGIGI. His color is the darkest black. His Essence is to be found in lead, in the burnt embers of the fire, and in things of death and of antiquity. The horns of a stag are his symbol. His Gate is the Last you will come upon in the rites that follow. His Step on the Ladder of Lights is Black.

This is his Seal, which you must engrave on a leaden plate or bowl, keeping it well hidden from the eyes of the profane. It should be wrapped and put away as all the others, until its use is desired. It should never be removed when the Sun is in the sky, but only after the night has fallen and the earth grown black, for NINIB knows best the ways of the demons that prowl among the shadows, looking for sacrifice. He knows best the territories of the Ancient Ones, the practices of their worshippers, and the locations of the Gates. His realm is the realm of the Night of Time.

His Number is Four, as the quarters of the Earth, and the following is his Seal:

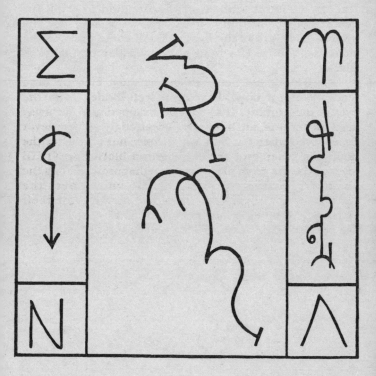

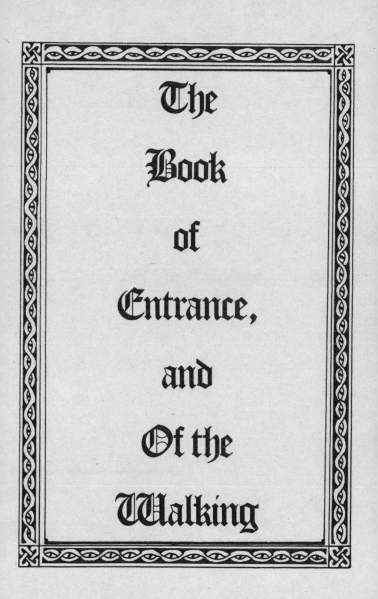

The

Book

of

Entrance,

and

Of the

Walking

THE BOOK OF ENTRANCE

THIS is the Book of Entrance to the Seven Zones above the Earth, which Zones were known to the Chaldeans, and to the ancient races that preceded them among the lost temples of UR. Know that these Zones are governed by the celestial spirits, and that passage may be had by the Priest through those lands that border on the Unzoned Wastes beyond. Know that, when Walking thus through the Sea of Spheres, he should leave his Watcher behind that It may guard his body and his property, lest he be slain unawares and must wander throughout eternity among the dark spaces between the Stars, or else be devoured by the wrathful IGIGI that dwell beyond.

Know that thou must Walk the Steps of the Ladder of Lights, each in its place and one at a time, and that thou must enter by the Gates in the lawful manner, as is put down in the Covenant; else, thou art surely lost.

Know that thou must keep purified for the space of one moon for the Entrance to the first Step, one moon between the First and the Second Step, and again between the Second and the Third, and so on in like manner. Thou must abstain from spilling thy seed in any manner for like period of time, but thou mayest worship at the Temple of ISHTAR, provided thou lose not thine Essence. And this is a great secret.

Thou must needs call upon thy God in the dawn light and upon thy Goddess in the light of dusk, every day of the moon of purification. Thou must summon thy Watcher and instruct it perfectly in its duties, providing it with a time and a place whereby it may serve thee and surround thee with a flaming sword, in every direction.

Thy clothing for the Walking should be fair, clean and simple, but appropriate to each Step. And thou should have with thee the Seal of the particular Step whereupon thou Walkest, which is the Seal of the Star appertaining thereunto.

Thou must needs prepare an altar to face the North, having upon it the statues of thine deities, or some such suitable Images, an offering bowl, and a brazier. Upon the earth should be inscribed the Gate appropriate to the Walking. If above thee is the Sky, so much the better. If there be a roof above thine head, it must be free from all hangings. Not even a lamp should be suspended over thee, save in Operations of Calling, which is discussed elsewhere (if the Gods grant me the time!). The only light shall be from the four lamps upon the ground, at each of the four Gates of the Earth: of the North, one lamp; of the East, one lamp; of the South, one lamp; and of the West, one lamp. The oil should be pure, with no odor, or else sweet-smelling. The perfumes in the brazier should also be sweet-smelling, or especially appropriate to the Star where thou wouldst desire Entrance, after the fashion of thy country.

The Seven Gates here follow:

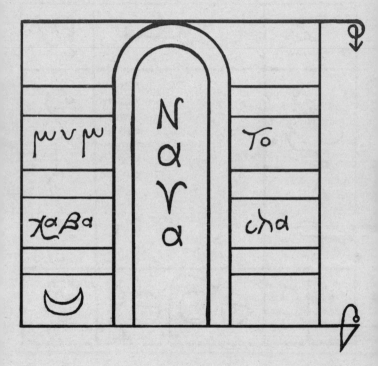

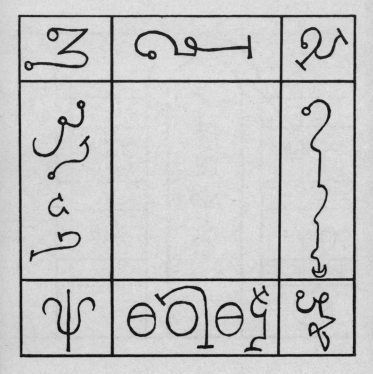

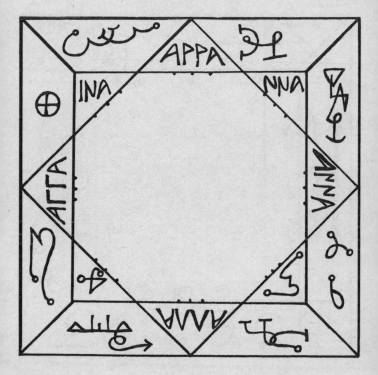

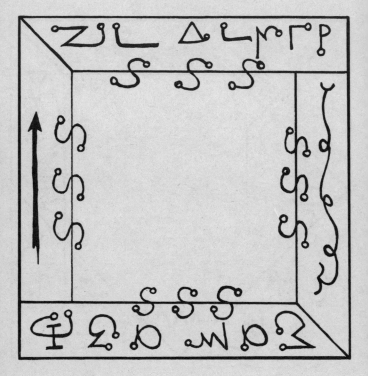

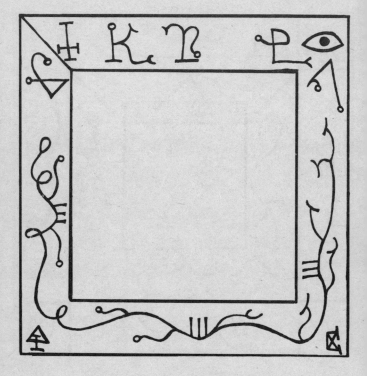

And the Ritual of the Walking must follow the formulae herein described:

First, thou must observe the moon of purification. In this time, thou mayest not eat meat for the space of seven days preceding the last day of the moon, and for the space of three days preceding the last day of the moon thou mayest not eat anything whatsoever, save to drink sweet water. On the last three days, thou must invoke, in addition to thy God and Goddess, the Three Great Elder Ones, ANU, ENLIL, ENKI, by their proper invocations. And the Number of ANU is Sixty, the Perfect Number, for he is Father of the Heavens. And the Number of ENLIL is Fifty, and he is the Father of the Wind. And the Number of ENKI is Forty a most excellent Number, and he is our Father, of all who would tread these forgotten paths, and wander into Lands unknown, among the Wastes, amid frightful monsters of the Azonei.

Second, on the Night of the Walking, which must be the thirteenth night of the moon, having begun on the previous thirteenth night, thou must approach the Gate with awe and respect. Thy Temple is exorcised. Thou must light the Fire and conjure it, by the invocation of the God of the Fire, and pour incense thereon. Thou must make offering to the Deities on the altar.

Third, thou must light the four lamps from the flaming brazier, reciting the invocation proper to each of these Watchtowers in its proper place, summoning the respective Star.

Fourth, thou must recite the invocation of the Watcher, thrusting the Sword into the Earth at Its station, not touching it until it is the appointed time for Its departure.

Fifth, thou must take the Seal of the Star in thy right hand, and whisper its Name softly upon it.

Sixth, thou must recite the Incantation of the

Walking, loudly, and in a clear voice, as thou walkest about the Gate in a circular fashion, beginning at the North and walking to the East, then to the South, and to the West, the Number of times being equal to the special Number of the Star.

Seventh, thou must needs arrive back at the center of the Gate, before thine altar, at which time thou must fall to the ground, looking neither to the right nor to the left at what may be moving there, for these Operations attract many kinds of wandering demon and ghost to the Gates, but in the air above the altar whereupon thou wilt presently see the Gate opening for thee and the Spirit-Messenger of the Sphere greeting thee in a clear voice, and giving thee a Name, which thou must remember, for that is the Name of thy Passing the Gate, which thou must use each time thou passeth thereby. The same Spirit-Messenger will meet thee and, if thou know not thy Name, he will forbid thee entrance and thou wilt fall to the Earth immediately.

When the First Gate has been entered and the Name received, thou wilt fall back to Earth amid thine Temple. That which has been moving about thy Gate on the ground will have gone. Recite thine thanksgiving to the Gods upon thine altar, strike the Sword of the Watcher that It may depart, and give the incantation of INANNA which says how she conquered the realm of the Underworld and vanquisheth KUTULU. All Idimmu will vanish thereby and thou wilt be thus free to depart the Gate and extinguish the Fire.

Thou mayest not call upon NANNA till thou hast passed the Gate of NANNA. Thou mayest not call NEBO until his Gate hast thou passed. Similarly for the rest of the Gates. When thou hast ascended to the limit of the Ladder of Lights, thou wilt have knowledge and power over the Spheres, and wilt be able to summon them thereby in times of need. This will not give thee power over the ABSU, however, this power being obtained differently by the Ritual of Descent. This Ritual thou wilt undertake in the fifteenth day after the thirteenth of the month when thou hast summoned the Gate of MARDUK to open. For MARDUK slew the Fiends, and INANNA, the Goddess of the Fifteen, conquered the Netherworld, where some of theirs still dwell. This is a most perilous Rite, and may be undertaken by any man who has the formulae, whether he has passed the previous Gates or not, save that it is best advised to have passed through MARDUK Gate before venturing forth into the Pit. For this reason, few have ever opened the Gate of ADAR, and spoken to the Horned One who resideth there and giveth all manner of wisdom regarding the operations of necromancy, and of the spells that hasten unto death. Only when thou hast shown thy power over the Maskim and the Rabishu, mayest thou venture forth to the Land of the IGIGI, and for that reason was this Covenant made, that none shall safely Walk through the sunken valleys of the Dead before having ascended to MARDUK, nor shall they breach the Gates that lie beyond ADAR until they have seen the Signs of the Mad God and felt the fury of the hellish Queen.

And against the Ancient Ones, there is only defence. Only a madman, indeed, such as I am called!, can hope to have power over Them that dwell in the Outer Spaces, for their power is unknown, and the number of their hordes uncounted, and each day they breed more horrors than a man's mind can conceive, the sight of which he can hardly bear. There was a time when the Gate to the Outside was open too long and I witnessed the horror that struck, of which words cannot speak, and of which writing can only confuse. The Ancient One that had escaped into the Inner World was forced back through the Gate by a magician of great power, but only at a great loss to the villages and flocks of the Island. Many sheep were slain after an unnatural fashion, and many devoured, and many Bedou rendered senseless; for the mind perceives what it is shown, but the sight of the Ancient Ones is a blasphemy to the ordinary senses of a man, for they come from a world that is not straight, but crooked, and their existence is of forms unnatural and painful to the eye and to the mind, whereby the spirit is threatened and wrenches loose from the body in flight. And for that reason, the fearful utukku xul take possession of the body and dwell therein until the Priest banish them back to whence they came, and the normal spirit may return to its erstwhile neighborhood.

And there are the ALLU, frightening dog-faced demons that are the Messengers of the Gods of Prey, and that chew on the very bones of a man. And there are many another, of which this is not the rightful place wherein they may be mentioned, save to warn the Priest against ambitious striving against the Ancient Ones of the Outside, until mastery is acquired over the powers that reside Within. Only when ADAR has been obtained, may the Priest consider himself a master over the planes of the Spheres, and able to wrestle with the Old Gods. Once Death Herself has been stared in the Eye, can the Priest then summon and control the denizens of Death's darkly curtained halls. Then can he hope to open the Gate without fear and without that loathing of the spirit that slays the man.

Then can he hope to have power over the demons that plague the mind and the body, pulling at the hair and grasping at the hands, and screaming vile Names into the airs of the Night.

For what comes on the Wind can only be slain by he who knows the Wind; and what comes on the seas can only be slain by he who knows Waters. Thus is it written, in the Ancient Covenant.

The

Incantations

of

The

Gates

THE INVOCATION OF THE NANNA GATE

Spirit of the Moon, Remember!
NANNA, Father of the Astral Gods, Remember!
In the Name of the Covenant sworn between Thee and
    the Race of Men,
I call to Thee! Hearken, and Remember!
From the Gates of the Earth, I call Thee! From the Four
    Gates of the Land KI, I pray to Thee!
O Lord, Hero of the Gods, who in heaven and upon the
    earth is exalted!
Lord NANNA, of the Race of ANU, hear me!
Lord NANNA, called SIN, hear me!
Lord NANNA, Father of the Gods of UR, hear me!
Lord NANNA, God of the Shining Crown of Night, hear
    me!
Maker of Kings, Progenitor of the Land, Giver of the
    Gilded Sceptre,
Hear me and Remember!
Mighty Father, Whose thought is beyond the comprehen-
    sion of gods and men,
Hear me and Remember!
Gate of the Great Gates of the Spheres, open unto me!
Master of the IGIGI, swing open Thy Gate!
Master of the ANNUNAKI, open the Gate to the Stars!
IA NAMRASIT! IA SIN! IA NANNA!
BASTAMAAGANASTA IA KIA KANPA!
MAGABATHI-YA NANNA KANPA!
MASHRITA NANNA ZIA KANPA!
IA MAG! IA GAMAG! IA ZAGASTHENA KIA!
ASHTAG KARELLIOSH!

THE INVOCATION OF THE NEBO GATE

Spirit of the Swift Planet, Remember!

NEBO, Custodian of the Gods, Remember!

NEBO, Father of the Sacred Writing, Remember!

In the Name of the Covenant sworn between Thee and the Race of Men,

I call to Thee! Hearken, and Remember!

From the Gate of the Great God NANNA, I call to Thee!

By the Name which I was given on the Lunar Sphere, I call to Thee!

Lord NEBO, who does not know of Thy Wisdom?

Lord NEBO, who does not know of Thy Magick?

Lord NEBO, what spirit, on earth or in the heavens, is not conjured by Thy mystic Writing?

Lord NEBO, what spirit, on earth or in the heavens, is not compelled by the Magick of Thy spells?

NEBO KURIOS! Lord of the Subtle Arts, Open the Gate to the Sphere of Thy Spirit!

NEBO KURIOS! Master of the Chemical Science, Open the Gate to the Sphere of Thy Workings!

Gate of the Swift Planet, MERKURIOS, Open unto me!

IA ATHZOTHTU! IA ANGAKU! IA ZI NEBO!

MARZAS ZI FORNIAS KANPA!

LAZHAKAS SHIN TALSAS KANPA!

NEBOS ATHANATOS KANPA!

IA GAASH! IA SAASH! IA KAKOLOMANI-YASH!

IA MAAKALLI!

THE INVOCATION OF THE ISHTAR GATE

Spirit of Venus, Remember!

ISHTAR, Mistress of the Gods, Remember!

ISHTAR, Queen of the Land of the Rising of the Sun, Remember!

Lady of Ladies, Goddess of Goddesses, ISHTAR, Queen of all People, Remember!

O Bright Rising, Torch of the Heaven and of Earth, Remember!

O Destroyer of the Hostile Hordes, Remember!

Lioness, Queen of the Battle, Hearken and Remember!

From the Gate of the Great God NEBO, I call Thee!

By the Name which I was given on the Sphere of NEBO, I call to Thee!

Lady, Queen of Harlots and of Soldiers, I call to Thee!

Lady, Mistress of Battle and of Love, I pray Thee, Remember!

In the Name of the Covenant, sworn between Thee and the Race of Men,

I call to Thee! Hearken and Remember!

Suppressor of the Mountains!

Supporter of arms!

Deity of Men! Goddess of Women! Where Thou gazest, the Dead live!

ISHTAR, Queen of Night, Open Thy Gate to me!

ISHTAR, Lady of the Battle, Open wide Thy Gate!

ISHTAR, Sword of the People, Open Thy Gate to me!

ISHTAR, Lady of the Gift of Love, Open wide Thy Gate!

Gate of the Gentle Planet, LIBAT, Open unto me!

IA GUSHE-YA! IA INANNA! IA ERNINNI-YA!

ASHTA PA MABACHA CHA KUR ENNI-YA!
RABBMI LO-YAK ZI ISHTARI KANPA!
INANNA ZI AMMA KANPA! BI ZAMMA KANPA!
IA IA IA BE -YI RAZULUKI!

THE INVOCATION OF THE SHAMMASH GATE

Spirit of the Sun, Remember!

SHAMMASH, Lord of the Fiery Disk, Remember!

In the Name of the Covenant sworn between Thee and
    Race of Men,

I call to Thee! Hearken and Remember!

From the Gate of the Beloved ISHTAR, the Sphere of
    LIBAT, I call to Thee!

Illuminator of Darkness, Destroyer of Evil, Lamp of
    Wisdom, I call to Thee! SHAMMASH, Bringer of
    Light, I call to Thee!

KUTULU is burned by Thy Might! AZAG-THOTH is
    fallen off His Throne before Thee! ISHNIGARRAB
    is scorched black by Thy rays!

Spirit of the Burning Disk, Remember!

Spirit of the Never-Ending Light, Remember!

Spirit of the Rending of the Veils of the Night, Dispeller
    of Darkness, Remember!

Spirit of the Opening of the Day, Open wide Thy Gate!

Spirit Who rises between the Mountains with splendour,
    Open Thy Gate to me!

By the Name which I was given on the Sphere of
    ISHTAR, I ask Thy Gate to open!

Gate of the Sun, Open to me!
Gate of the Golden Sceptre, Open to me!
Gate of the Life-Giving Power, Open! Open!
IA UDDU-YA! IA RUSSULUXI!
SAGGTAMARANIA! IA! IA! ATZARACHI-YA!
ATZARELECHI-YU! BARTALAKATAMANI-YA KANPA!
ZI DINGIR UDDU-YA KANPA! ZI DINGIR USHTU-YA
      KANPA!
ZI SHTA! ZI DARAKU! ZI BELURDUK!
KANPA! IA SHTA KANPA! IA!

THE INVOCATION OF THE NERGAL GATE

Spirit of the Red Planet, Remember!
NERGAL, God of War, Remember!
NERGAL, Vanquisher of Enemies, Commander of Hosts,
      Remember!
NERGAL, Slayer of Lions and of Men, Remember!
In the Name of the Covenant sworn between Thee and
      the Race of Men,
I call to Thee! Hearken, and Remember!
From the Great Gate of the Lord SHAMMASH, the
      Sphere of the Sun,
I call to Thee!
NERGAL, God of the Sacrifice of Blood, Remember!
NERGAL, Lord of the Offerings of Battle, Ravager of the
      Enemy's Towns,
Devourer of the flesh of Man, Remember!
NERGAL, Wielder of the Mighty Sword, Remember!

NERGAL, Lord of Arms and Armies, Remember!

Spirit of the Glow of the Battlefield, Open wide Thy Gate!

Spirit of the Entrance Unto Death, Open Thy Gate to me!

Spirit of the Sailing Lance, the Thrusting Sword, the Flying Rock,

Open the Gate to Thy Sphere to One who has no fear!

Gate of the Red Planet, Open!

Gate of the God of War, Swing wide!

Gate of the God of Victory got in Battle, Open to me!

Gate of the Lord of Protection, Open!

Gate of the Lord of the ARRA and the AGGA, Open!

By the Name which I was given on the Sphere of SHAMMASH, I ask Thee, Open!

IA NERGAL-YA! IA ZI ANNGA KANPA!

IA NNGA! IA NNGR-YA! IA! NNGYA! IA ZI DINGIR NEENYA KANPA!

IA KANTALAMAKKYA TARRA! KANPA!

THE INVOCATION OF THE MARDUK GATE

Spirit of the Great Planet, Remember!

MARDUK, God of Victory Over the Dark Angels, Remember!

MARDUK, Lord of All the Lands, Remember!

MARDUK, Son of ENKI, Master of Magicians, Remember!

MARDUK, Vanquisher of the Ancient Ones, Remember!

MARDUK, Who gives the Stars their Powers, Remember!

MARDUK, Who assigns the Wanderers their Places, Remember!

Lord of the Worlds, and of The Spaces Between, Remember!

First among the Astral Gods, Hearken and Remember!

In the Name of the Covenant sworn between Thee and the Race of Men,

I call to Thee! Hearken and Remember!

From the Gate of the Mighty NERGAL, the Sphere of the Red Planet,

I call to Thee! Hearken and Remember!

MARDUK, Lord of The Fifty Powers, Open Thy Gates to me!

MARDUK, God of Fifty Names, Open Thy Gates to Thy Servant!

By the Name which I was given on the Sphere of NERGAL, I call to Thee to Open!

Gate of the Great God, Open!

Gate of the God of the Double-Headed Axe, Open!

Gate of the Lord of the World Between the Worlds, Open!

Gate of the Conqueror of the Monsters from the Sea, Open!

Gate of the Golden City of SAGALLA, Open!

IA DAG! IA GAT! IA MARGOLQBABBONNESH!

IA MARRUTUKKU! IA TUKU! SUHRIM SUHGURIM!

ZAHRIM ZAHGURIM! AXXANNGABANNAXAXAGAN-NABABILLUKUKU!

THE INVOCATION OF THE NINIB GATE

Spirit of the Wanderer of the Wastes, Remember!
Spirit of the Planet of Time, Remember!
Spirit of the Planet of the Hunter, Remember!
NINIB, Lord of the Dark Ways, Remember!
NINIB, Lord of the Secret Passages, Remember!
NINIB, Knower of the Secrets of All Things, Remember!
NINIB, Knower of the Ways of the Ancient Ones,
    Remember!
NINIB, Horned One of Silence, Remember!
NINIB, Watcher of the Ways of the IGIGI, Remember!
NINIB, Knower of the Pathways of the Dead, Remember!
In the Name of the Covenant sworn between Thee and
    the Race of Men,
I call to Thee! Hearken and Remember!
From the Mighty Gate of the Lord of the Gods,
    MARDUK, Sphere of the Great Planet,
I call to Thee! Hearken and Remember!
NINIB, Dark Wanderer of the Forgotten Lands, Hearken
    and Remember!
NINIB, Gatekeeper of the Astral Gods, Open Thy Gate to
    me!
NINIB, Master of the Chase and the Long Journey, Open
    Thy Gate to me!
Gate of the Double-Horned Elder God, Open!
Gate of the Last City of the Skies, Open!
Gate of the Secret of All Time, Open!
Gate of the Master of Magickal Power, Open!
Gate of the Lord of All Sorcery, Open!

Gate of the Vanquisher of all Evil Spells, Hearken and
   Open!
By the Name which I was given on the Sphere of
   MARDUK, Master of Magicians,
I call Thee to Open!
IA DUK! IA ANDARRA! IA ZI BATTU BA ALLU!
BALLAGU BEL DIRRIGU BAAGGA KA KANPA!
BEL ZI EXA EXA!
AZZAGBAT! BAZZAGBARRONIOSH!
ZELIG!

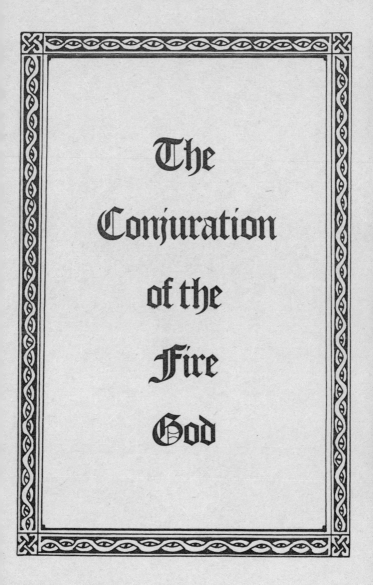

The

Conjuration

of the

Fire

God

THE CONJURATION OF THE FIRE GOD

Spirit of the Fire, Remember!

GIBIL, Spirit of the Fire, Remember!

GIRRA, Spirit of the Flames, Remember!

O God of Fire, Mighty Son of ANU, Most terrifying among
    Thy Brothers,

Rise!

O God of the Furnace, God of Destruction, Remember!

Rise Up, O God of Fire, GIBIL in Thy Majesty, and
    devour my enemies!

Rise up, O God of Fire, GIRRA in Thy Power, and burn
    the sorcerers who persecute me!

GIBIL GASHRU UMUNA YANDURU

TUSHTE YESH SHIR ILLANI U MA YALKI!

GISHBAR IA ZI IA

IA ZI DINGIR GIRRA KANPA!

Rise up, Son of the Flaming Disk of ANU!

Rise up, Offspring of the Golden Weapon of MARDUK!

It is not I, but ENKI, Master of the Magicians, who
    summons Thee!

It is not I, but MARDUK, Slayer of the Serpent, who calls
    Thee here now!

Burn the Evil and the Evildoer!

Burn the Sorcerer and the Sorceress!

Singe them! Burn them! Destroy them!

Consume their powers!

Carry them away!

Rise up, GISHBAR BA GIBBIL BA GIRRA ZI AGA
    KANPA!

Spirit of the God of Fire, Thou art Conjured!

KAKKAMMANUNU!

The
Conjuration
of the
Watcher

THIS is the Book of the Conjuration of the Watcher, the formulae as I received them from the Scribe of ENKI, Our Master and Lord of All Magick. Great care must be taken that this untame Spirit does not rise up against the Priest, and for that reason a preliminary sacrifice must be made in a clean and new bowl with the appropriate sigils inscribed thereupon, being the three grey carven signs of the Rock of my initiation, which are:

They must be engraved upon the bowl with a fine stylus, or painted thereon with dark ink. The sacrifice must be new bread, pine resin, and the grass Olieribos. These must be burned in the new bowl, and the Sword of the Watcher, with his Sigil engraved thereupon, at hand, for he will inhabit such at the time of the Calling of the Watcher and will depart when he is given license to depart.

The Watcher comes from a Race different from

that of Men and yet different from that of the Gods, and it is said that he was with KINGU and his hordes at the time of the War between the Worlds, but was dissatisfied and did cleave unto the Armies of Lord MARDUK.

Wherefore it is wise to conjur It in the Names of the Three Great Watchers Who existed before the Confrontation, from whose borne the Watcher and His Race ultimately derive, and those Three are ANU, ENLIL, and Master ENKI of the Magick Waters. And for this reason They are sometimes called the Three Watchers, MASS SSARATI and the Watcher MASS SSARATU, or KIA MASS SSARATU.

And the Watcher appears sometimes as a great and fierce Dog, who prowls about the Gate or the Circle, frightening away the idimmu who forever lurk about the barriers, waiting for sacrifice. And the Watcher sometimes appears as a great and noble Spirit, holding aloft the Sword of Flames, and even the Elder Gods are awed thereby. And sometimes the Watcher appears as a Man in a Long Robe, shaven, with eyes that never lose their stare. And the Lord of the Watchers dwells, it is said, among the Wastes of the IGIGI, and only Watches and never raises the Sword or fights the idimmi, save when the Covenant is invoked by none less than the Elder Gods in their Council, like unto the Seven Glorious APHKHALLU.

And sometimes the Watcher appears as the Enemy, ready to devour the Priest who has erred in the incantations, or omitted the sacrifice, or acted in defiance of the Covenant, for which acts the very Elder Gods cannot forbid that silent Race from exacting its toll. And it is said that some of that Race lie waiting for the Ancient Ones to once more rule the Cosmos, that they may be given the right hand of honor, and that such as these are lawless. This is what is said.

When the time has come to summon the Watcher the first time, the place of thy calling must be clean, and a double circle of flour drawn about thee. And there should be no altar, but only the new Bowl with the three carven signs on it. And the Conjuration of the Fire should be made, and the sacrifices heaped thereupon, into the burning bowl. And the Bowl is now called AGA MASS SSARATU, and to be used for no other purpose, save to invoke the Watcher.

And the bowl must be lain between the Circles, facing the Northeast.

And thy vestments should be black, and thy cap black.

And the Sword must be at hand, but not yet in the ground.

And it must be the Darkest Hour of the Night.

And there must be no light, save for the AGA MASS SSARATU.

And the Conjuration of the Three must be made, thus:

ISS MASS SSARATI SHA MUSHI LIPSHURU RUXI-SHA LIMNUTI!

IZIZANIMMA ILANI RABUTI SHIMA YA DABABI!

DINI DINA ALAKTI LIMDA!

ALSI KU NUSHI ILANI MUSHITI!

IA MASS SSARATI ISS MASS SSARATI BA IDS MASS SSARATU!

And this special Conjuration may be made at any time the Priest feels he is in danger, whether his life or his spirit, and the Three Watchers and the One Watcher will rush to his aid.

This being said, at the words IDS MASS SSARATU the Sword must be thrust into the ground behind the AGA MASS SSARATU with force. And the Watcher will appear for the instructions to be made by the Priest.

THE NORMAL INVOCATION OF THE WATCHER

This Invocation is to be made during the course of any Ceremony when it is necessary to summon the Watcher to preside over the outer precincts of the Circle or Gate. The Sword is to be thrust into the ground as before, in the Northeast section, but the AGA MASS SSARATU is not necessary LEST THOU HAST NOT MADE SACRIFICE TO THINE WATCHER IN THE SPACE OF ONE MOON in which case it is necessary to sacrifice to It anew, whether in that Ceremony or at some other, earlier.

Raise the Copper Dagger of INANNA of the Calling, and declaim the Invocation in a clear voice, be it loud or soft:

IA MASS SSARATU!
I conjure Thee by the Fire of GIRRA
The Veils of Sunken Varloorni,
And by the Lights of SHAMMASH.
I call Thee here, before me, in visible shadow
In beholdable Form, to Watch and Protect this Sacred
    Circle, this Holy Gate of (N.)
May He of the Name Unspeakable, the Number
    Unknowable,
Whom no man hath seen at any time,
Whom no geometer measureth
Whom no wizard hath ever called

CALL THEE HERE NOW!
Rise up, by ANU I summon Thee!
Rise up, by ENLIL I summon Thee!
Rise up, by ENKI I summon Thee!
Cease to be the Sleeper of EGURRA.
Cease to lie unwaking beneath the Mountains of KUR.
Rise up, from the pits of ancient holocausts!
Rise up, from the old Abyss of NARR MARRATU!
Come, by ANU!
Come, by ENLIL!
Come, by ENKI!
In the Name of the Covenant, Come and Rise up before
    me!

IA MASS SSARATU! IA MASS SSARATU! IA MASS
    SSARATU ZI KIA KANPA!
BARRGOLOMOLONETH KIA!
SHTAH!

        At this point, the Watcher will surely come and
will stand outside the Gate or Circle until such time as
he is given the license to depart by the striking of the
Priest's left hand on the hilt of the Sword, while
pronouncing the formula BARRA MASS SSARATU!
BARRA!
        Thou mayest not depart thine sacred precincts
until the Watcher has been given this license, else he will
devour thee. Such are the laws.
        And he care not what he Watches, only that he
obey the Priest.

The
MAKLU
Text

THE BOOK MAKLU
OF THE BURNING OF THE EVIL SPIRITS

ERE are the Banishments, the Burnings, and the Bindings handed down to us by ENKI, the Master. They are to be performed over the AGA MASS SSARATU by the Priest, with the appropriate images as described herein. The incantations must be recited after the Watcher has been summoned, and he will do the deeds set down for him by the incantations. When he returns, he is to be dismissed as set down previously. Know that, when images are used, they must be burned utterly, and the ashes buried in safe ground where none may find them, else to touch them would mean death.

Know that the Evil Spirits are principally Seven, for the Seven Maskim who tear away the heart of a man and mock his Gods. And their Magick is very strong, and they are the Lords over the shadows and over the depths of the Seas, and reigned once, it is said, over MAGAN, whence they came. The banishings, or exorcisms, are to be pronounced in a clear voice without trembling, without shaking. The arms should be held over the head in the attitude of a Priest of SHAMMASH, and the eyes must behold the Spirit of the God SHAMMASH, even though it be the time of the Sleeping of SHAMMASH behind the Mountains of the Scorpion.

No word must be changed. These must not be shown to any but the properly instructed. To show them to anyone Other is to ask the curse of NINNGHIZHIDA on yourself and upon your generations.

The Book MAKLU of the Burnings:

THE EXORCISM OF THE CROWN OF ANU

The Priest, in time of peril, shall put on the spotless white crown of ANU with the Eight-rayed Seal and stand in the prescribed manner with the Tablets of Calling on his breast and the copper Dagger of INANNA in his right hand, aloft.

For, it is said, if a man builds a fire, does he not build it in a Pit, that he might not be harmed thereby? Thus is it true of the UDUGGU we call, for they are like Fire and every caution must be used lest they consume the magician and his entire generation.

Thus, the Exorcism of ANU

I have put the Starry Crown of Heaven, the potent Disk
    of ANU on my head
That a kindly Spirit and a kindly Watcher
Like the God that hath made me
May stand at my head always
To lift me to favor with the Elder Gods
UDUGGHUL
ALLACHUL
GIDDIMCHUL
MALLACHUL
MASQIMCHUL
DINGIRCHUL

No Evil Spirit
No Evil Demon
No Evil God
No Evil Fiend
No Hag Demon
No Filth-Eating Demon
No Thieving Demon
No Shadow of the Night
No Shell of the Night
No Mistress of the Demon
No Offspring of the Demon
No Evil Spell
No Enchantment
No Sorcery
NO EVIL IN THE WORLD OR UNDER IT
OVER THE WORLD OR INSIDE THE WORLD
MAY SEIZE ME HERE!
BARRA ANTE MALDA!
BARRA ANGE GE YENE!
ZI DINGIR ANNA KANPA!
ZI DINGIR KIA KANPA!
GAGGAMANNU!

A CONJURATION AGAINST
THE SEVEN LIERS-IN-WAIT

They are Seven
They are Seven
In the depths of the ocean, they are Seven
In the shining heavens, they are Seven

They proceed from the ocean depths
They proceed from the hidden retreat
They are neither male nor female
These which stretch themselves out like chains
They have no spouse
They beget not children
They are strangers to charity
They ignore prayers
They scoff at wishes
They are vermin that come forth from the Mountains of
    MASHU
Enemies of Our Master ENKI
They are the vengeance of the Ancient Ones
Raising up difficulties
Obtaining power through wickedness
The Enemies! The Enemies! The Seven Enemies!
They are Seven!
They are Seven!
They are Seven times Seven!
Spirit of the Sky, Remember! Spirit of the Earth,
    Remember!

THE EXORCISM BARRA EDINNAZU
FOR SPIRITS WHO ATTACK THE CIRCLE

ZI ANNA KANPA!
ZI KIA KANPA!
GALLU BARRA!
NAMTAR BARRA!
ASHAK BARRA!
GIGIM BARRA!

ALAL BARRA!
TELAL BARRA!
MASQIM BARRA!
UTUQ BARRA!
IDPA BARRA!
LALARTU BARRA!
LALLASSU BARRA!
AKHKHARU BARRA!
URUKKU BARRA!
KIELGALAL BARRA!
LILITU BARRA!
UTUQ XUL EDIN NA ZU!
ALLA XUL EDIN NA ZU!
GIGIM XUL EDIN NA ZU!
MULLA XUL EDIN NA ZU!
DINGIRXUL EDIN NA ZU!
MASQIM XUL EDIN NA ZU!
BARRA!
EDINNAZU!
ZI ANNA KANPA! ZI KIA KANPA!

THE EXORCISM ZI DINGIR

(To be used against any kind of malefick)

ZI DINGIR NNGI E NE KANPA
ZI DINGIR NINGI E NE KANPA
ZI DINGIR ENNUL E NE KANPA
ZI DINGIR NINNUL E NE KANPA
ZI DINGIR ENN KURKUR E NE KANPA
ZI DINGIR NINN KURKUR E NE KANPA

ZI DINGIR N DA SHURRIM MA KANPA
ZI DINGIR NINNDA SHURRIM MA KANPA
ZI DINGIR ENDUL AAZAG GA KANPA
ZI DINGIR NINNDUL AAZAG GA KANPA
ZI DINGIR ENUHDDIL LA KANPA
ZI DINGIR NINN UHDDIL LA KANPA
ZI DINGIR ENMESHIR RAA KANPA
ZI DINGIR NINNME SHIR RAA KANPA
ZI DINGIR ENAA MAA A DINGIR ENLIL LAAGE
    KANPA
ZI DINGIR NINNA MAA A DINGIR NINNLIL LAAGE
    KANPA
ZI DINGIR SSISGI GISH MA SAGBA DAA NI IDDA
    ENNUBALLEMA KANPA
ZI DINGIR BHABBHAR L'GAL DEKUD DINGIR RI
    ENNEGE KANPA
ZI DINGIR NINNI DUGGAANI DINGIR A NNUNNA IA
    AN SAGGNNUUNGA GATHA GAN ENE KANPA!

THE EXORCISM AGAINST AZAG-THOTH
AND HIS EMISSARIES

(An image must be made of a throne-chair, and put into
the flames of the AGA MASS SSARATU while chanting
the following exorcism.)

Boil! Boil! Burn! Burn!
UTUK XUL TA ARDATA!
Who art thou, whose son?
Who art thou, whose daughter?
What sorcery, what spells, has brought thee here?

May ENKI, the Master of Magicians, free me!

May ASHARILUDU, son of ENKI, free me!

May they bring to nought your vile sorceries!

I chain you!

I bind you!

I deliver you to GIRRA

Lord of the Flames

Who sears, burns, enchains

Of whom even mighty KUTULU has fear!

May GIRRA, the Ever-burning One, give strength to my arms!

May GIBIL, the Lord of Fire, give power to my Magick!

Injustice, murder, freezing of the loins,

Rending of the bowels, devouring of the flesh, and madness

In all ways hast thou persecuted me!

Mad God of CHAOS!

May GIRRA free me!

AZAG-THOTH TA ARDATA! IA MARDUK! IA MARDUK! IA ASALLUXI!

You have chosen me for a corpse.

You have delivered me to the Skull.

You have sent Phantoms to haunt me.

You have sent vampires to haunt me.

To the wandering Ghosts of the Wastes, have you delivered me.

To the Phantoms of the fallen ruins, have you delivered me.

To the deserts, the wastes, the forbidden lands, you have handed me over.

Open Thy Mouth In Sorceries Against Me No More!
I have handed thine image over
Into the flames of GIBIL!
Burn, Mad Fiend!
Boil, Mad God!
May the Burning GIRRA untie thy knots!
May the Flames of GIBIL untie your cord!
May the Law of the Burning seize your throat!
May the Law of the Burning avenge me!

It is not I, but MARDUK, son of ENKI, Masters in Magick,
    that commands Thee!

KAKKAMMU! KANPA!

INCANTATION AGAINST THE ANCIENT ONES

(To be recited each year, when the Bear hangs from its
Tail in the Heavens)

Destructive Storms and Evil Winds are they
An evil blast, herald of the baneful storm
An evil blast, forerunner of the baneful storm
They are mighty children, Ancient Ones
Heralds of Pestilence
Throne-bearers of NINNKIGAL
They are the flood which rusheth through the Land

Seven Gods of the Broad Heavens
Seven Gods of the Broad Earth
Seven Ancient Ones are They

Seven Gods of Might
Seven Evil Gods
Seven Evil Demons
Seven Demons of Oppression
Seven in Heaven
Seven on Earth

UTUG XUL
ALA XUL
GIDIM XUL
MULLA XUL
DINGIR XUL
MASQIM XUL
ZI ANNA KANPA!
ZI KIA KANPA
ZI DINGIR ENLIL LA LUGAL KURKUR RA GE KANPA!
ZI DINGIR NINLIL LA NIN KURKUR RA GE KANPA!
ZI DINGIR NINIB IBILA ESHARRA GE KANPA!
ZI DINGIR NINNI NIN KURKUR RA GE KANPA!
ZI DINGIR A NUNNA DINGIR GALGALLA E NE
    KANPA!
ZI DINGIR ANNA KANPA!
ZI DINGIR KIA KANPA!

BABABARARARA ANTE MALDADA!
BABABARARARA ANTE GEGE ENENE!

INCANTATION OF PROTECTION
AGAINST THE WORKERS OF THE ANCIENT ONES

SHAMMASH SHA KASHSHAPIYA KASSHAP TIYA
   EPISHYA MUSHTEPISH TIYA!
   Kima Tinur khuturshunu l'rim!
   Lichulu Lizubu u Littaattuku!
   E Pishtashunu Kima meh naadu ina tikhi likhtu!

SHUNU LIMUTUMA ANAKU LU'UBLUYI!
SHUNU LINISHUMA ANAKU LU'UDNIN!
SHUNU LI'IKTISHUMA ANAKU LUUPPATAR!
   Tirrama shaluti Sha Kashshapti Sha Ruchi ye
   Ipushu
   Shupi yi arkhish Uppu yush!
ZI DINGIR GAL KESHSHEBA KANPA!

(This to be recited Seven times in the Circle of Flour
before the AGA MASS SSARATU when it is found that
the worshippers of TIAMAT are raising Powers against
thee or thy neighborhood. Or, it may said when the Great
Bear is suspended from his Tail in the Heavens, which is
the Time the baneful worshippers gather for their Rites,
and by which they mark their calendar. The mercy of
ANU be upon thee!)

THE EXORCISM AGAINST THE POSSESSING SPIRIT

(This to be said when the body of the possessed is
distant, or when secrecy must be maintained. To be
performed within thy Circle, before the Watcher.)

The wicked God
The wicked Demon
The Demon of the Desert
The Demon of the Mountain
The Demon of the Sea
The Demon of the Marsh
The wicked Genius
The Enormous Larvae
The wicked Winds
The Demon that seizeth the body
The Demon that rendeth the body
SPIRIT OF THE SKY, REMEMBER!
SPIRIT OF THE EARTH, REMEMBER!

The Demon that seizeth man
The Demon that seizeth man
The GIGIM who worketh Evil
The Spawn of the wicked Demon
SPIRIT OF THE SKY, REMEMBER!
SPIRIT OF THE EARTH, REMEMBER!

He who forges images
He who casts spells
The Evil Angel
The Evil Eye
The Evil Mouth
The Evil Tongue
The Evil Lip
The Most Perfect Sorcery
SPIRIT OF THE SKY, REMEMBER!
SPIRIT OF THE EARTH, REMEMBER!

NINNKIGAL, Spouse of NINNAZU
May she cause him to turn his face toward the Place
    where she is!
May the wicked Demons depart!
May they seize one another!
May they feed on one another's bones!
SPIRIT OF THE SKY, REMEMBER!
SPIRIT OF THE EARTH, REMEMBER!

THE EXORCISM ANNAKIA

(A conjuration of Heaven and Earth and All Between
against the Possessing Spirit, to be recited seven times
over the body of the possessed person till the spirit
issueth forth from his nose and mouth in the form of
liquid and fire, like unto green oils. Then the person
shall be whole, and shall sacrifice to INANNA at her
Temple. And this must not be omitted, lest the spirit
return to what INANNA has cast off.)

ZI DINGIR ANNA KANPA!
ZI DINGIR KIA KANPA!
ZI DINGIR URUKI KANPA!
ZI DINGIR NEBO KANPA!
ZI DINGIR ISHTAR KANPA!
ZI DINGIR SHAMMASH UDDU KANPA!
ZI DINGIR NERGAL KANPA!
ZI DINGIR MARDUK KANPA!
ZI DINGIR NINIB ADDAR KANPA!
ZI DINGIR IGIGI KANPA!
ZI DINGIR ANNUNNAKIA KANPA!

ZI DINGIR ENLIL LA LUGAL KURKURRAGE KANPA!
ZI DINGIR NENLIL LA NINKURKURRAGE KANPA!
ZI DINGIR NINIB IBBILA ESHARRAGE KANPA!
ZI DINGIR NINNININ KURKURRAGE GIGSHI INN
    BHABBHARAGE KANPA!
ZI DINGIR ANNUNNA DINGIR GALGALLAENEGE
    KANPA!
KAKAMMU!

THE BINDING OF THE EVIL SORCERERS

(When thou art haunted by the spells of the worshippers
of the Ancient Ones, make images of them, one male and
one female, and burn them in the flames of the AGA
MASS SSARATU, while pronouncing the following
Incantation of the Binding:)

I invoke you, Gods of the Night
Together with you I call to the Night, to the Covered
    Woman
I call in the Evening, at Midnight, and in the Morning
Because they have enchanted me
The sorcerer and the sorceress have bound me
My God and my Goddess cry over me.
I am plagued with pain because of illness.
I stand upright, I cannot lie down
Neither during the night nor during the day.
They have stuffed my mouth with cords!
They have closed my mouth with grass!
They have made the water of my drink scarce.
My joy is sorrow, and my merriment is grief.

Arise! Great Gods! Hear my wailing!

Obtain justice! Take notice of my Ways!

I have an image of the sorcerer and the sorceress,

Of my enchanter and enchantress.

May the Three Watches of the Night dissolve their evil
    sorceries!

May their mouths be wax, their tongues honey.

The word of my doom which they have spoken,

May they melt like wax!

The spell that they worked, may it pour away like honey.

Their knot is broken!

Their work destroyed!

All their speech fills the deserts and the wastes

According to the Decree which the Gods of the Night
    have issued.

It is finished.

ANOTHER BINDING OF THE SORCERERS

(Take a cord with ten knots. As you recite each line of the
incantation, untie one knot. When this is finished, throw
the cord into the flames and give thanks to the Gods)

My images have you given over to the dead; turn back!

My images have you seen with the dead; turn back!

My images have you thrown to the side of the dead; turn
    back!

My images have you thrown to the ground of the dead;
    turn back!

My images have you buried in the coffin with the dead; turn back!

My images have you given over to destruction; turn back!

My images have you enclosed with walls; turn back!

My images have you struck down on doorsteps; turn back!

My images have you locked into the gate of the wall; turn back!

My images have you given over to the God of Fire; turn back!

A MOST EXCELLENT CHARM AGAINST THE HORDES OF DEMONS THAT ASSAIL IN THE NIGHT

(May be chanted while walking around the circumference of the Circle, and sprinkling the vicinity with sweet water, using a pine cone or golden brush. An image of a Fish may be at hand, and the incantation pronounced clearly, every word, either whispered softly, or shouted loudly.)

ISA YA! ISA YA! RI EGA! RI EGA!
BI ESHA BI ESHA! XIYILQA! XIYILQA!
DUPPIRA ATLAKA ISA YA U RI EGA
LIMUTTIKUNU KIMA QUTRI LITILLI SHAMI YE
INA ZUMRI YA ISA YA
INA ZUMRI YA RI EGA
INA ZUMRI YA BI ESHA
INA ZUMRI YA XIYILQA
INA ZUMRI YA DUPPIRA

INA ZUMRI YA ATLAKA
INA ZUMRI YA LA TATARA
INA ZUMRI YA LA TETIXXI YE
INA ZUMRI YA LA TAQARRUBA
INA ZUMRI YA LA TASANIQA
NI YISH SHAMMASH KABTU LU TAMATUNU
NI YISH ENKI BEL GIMRI LU TAMATUNU
NI YISH MARDUK MASHMASH ILANI LU TAMATUNU
NI YISH GISHBAR QAMIKUNU LU TAMATUNU
INA ZUMRI YA LU YU TAPPARRASAMA!

THE CONJURATION OF THE MOUNTAINS OF MASHU

(A spell to cause consternation in the Enemy, and
confuse his thoughts. It is also a binding, that the evil
sorcerer may not see his spells work their desired ends,
but melt away like honey or wax. These Mountains are
called SHADU, and are the hiding places of the Serpents
of KUR. A spell to cause ultimate destruction.)

SHADU YU LIKTUMKUNUSHI
SHADU YU LIKLAKUNUSHI
SHADU YU LINI YIX KUNUSHI
SHADU YU LI YIXSI KUNUSHI
SHADU YU LITE KUNUSHI
SHADU YU LINI KUNUSHI
SHADU YU LINIR KUNUSHI
SHADU YU LIKATTIN KUNUSHI
SHADU YU DANNU ELIKUNU LIMQUT
INA ZUMRI YA LU YU TAPPARRASAMA!

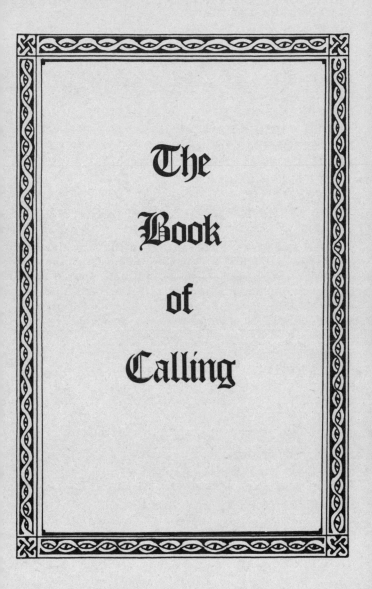

The

Book

of

Calling

THIS is the Book of the Ceremonies of Calling, handed down since the time the Elder Gods walked the Earth, Conquerors of the Ancient Ones.

This is the Book of NINNGHIZHIDDA, Horned Serpent, the Lady of the Magick Wand.

This is the Book of NINAXAKUDDU, The Queen, Mistress of the Incantations.

This is the Book of ASALLUXI, the King, the Lord of Magick.

This is the Book of AZAG, the Enchanter.

This is the Book of EGURA, the Dark Waters of ABSU, Realm of ERESHKIGAL, Queen of Death.

This is the Book of the Ministers of Knowledge, FIRIK and PIRIK, the Demon of the Snake-Entwined Magick Wand and the Demon of the Thunderbolt, Protectors of the Arcane Faith, the Most Secret Knowledge, to be hidden from those not of us, from the uninitiated.

This is the Book of ASARU, the Eye on the Throne.

This is the book of USHUMGALLUM, Mighty Dragon, born of HUBUR, of the Battle Against the Elder Gods.

This is the Book of ENDUKUGGA and NINDUKUGGA, Male and Female Monsters of the Abyss, of the Claws like Daggers and the Wings of Darkness.

This is further the Book of NAMMTAR, Chief among the Magicians of ERESHKIGAL.

This is the Book of the Seven Demons of the

Ignited Spheres, of the Seven Demons of the Flame.

This is the Book of the Priest, who governeth the Works of Fire!

Know, first, that the Power of the Conquerors is the Power of the Magick, and that the stricken gods will ever tempt thee away from the Legions of the Mighty, and that you will feel the subtle fluids of thy body moving to the breath of TIAMAT and the Blood of KINGU who races in your veins. Be ever watchful, therefore, not to open this Gate, or, if thou must needs, put a time for its closing before the rising of the Sun, and seal it at that time; for to leave it open is to be the agent of CHAOS.

Know, secondly, that the Power of Magick is the Power of Our Master ENKI, Lord of the Seas, and Master of Magick, Father of MARDUK, Fashioner of the Magick Name, the Magick Number, the Magick Word, the Magick Shape. So, therefore, the Priest who governeth the works of Fire, and of the God of Fire, GISHBAR called GIBIL, must firstly spinkle with the Water of the Seas of ENKI, as a testament to his Lordship and a sign of the Covenant that exists between him and thee.

Know, thirdly, that by the Power of the Elder Gods and the submission of the Ancient Ones, thou mayest procure every type of honor, dignity, wealth and happiness, but that these are to be shunned as the Purveyors of Death, for the most radiant jewels are to be found buried deep in the Earth, and the Tomb of Man is the Splendor of ERESHKIGAL, the joy of KUTULU, the food of AZAG-THOTH.

Therefore, thine obligation is as of the Gatekeeper of the Inside, agent of MARDUK, servant of ENKI, for the Gods are forgetful, and very far away, and it was to the Priests of the Flame that Covenant was given to seal the Gates between this World and the

Other, and to keep Watch thereby, through this Night of Time, and the Circle of Magick is the Barrier, the Temple, and the Gate between the Worlds.

Know, fourthly, that it is become the obligation of the Priests of the Flame and the Sword, and of all Magick, to bring their Power to the Underworld and keep it chained thereby, for the Underworld is surely the Gate Forgotten, by which the Ancient Ones ever seek Entrance to the Land of the Living. And the Ministers of ABSU are clearly walking the Earth, riding on the Air, and upon the Earth, and sailing silently through the Water, and roaring in the Fire, and all these Spirits must be brought to subjection to the Person of the Priest of Magick, before any else. Or the Priest becomes prey to the Eye of Death of the Seven ANNUNNAKI, Lords of the Underworld, Ministers of the Queen of Hell.

Know, fifthly, that the worshippers of TIAMAT are abroad in the world, and will give fight to the Magician. Lo, they have worshipped the Serpent from Ancient Times, and have always been with us. And they are to be known by their seeming human appearance which has the mark of the Beast upon them, as they change easily into the Shapes of animals and haunt the Nights of Men; and by their odor, which comes of burning incenses unlawful to the worship of the Elder Ones. And their Books are the Books of CHAOS and the flames, and are the Books of the Shadows and the Shells. And they worship the heaving earth and the ripping sky and the rampant flame and the flooding waters; and they are the raisers of the legions of maskim, the Liers-In-Wait. And they do not know what it is they do, but they do it at the demands of the Serpent, at whose Name even ERESHKIGAL gives fright, and the dread KUTULU strains at his bonds:

MUMMU TIAMAT Queen of the Ancient Ones!

Know, sixthly, that thou shalt not seek the operations of this Magick save by the rules and governments set down herein, for to do other is to take the most awful risk, for thyself and for all mankind. Therefore, heed these words carefully, and change not the words of the incantations, whether thou understand them, or understand them not, for they are the words of the Pacts made of Old, and before Time. So, say them softly if the formula is "softly", or shout them aloud if the formula is "aloud", but change not one measure lest thou call something Else, and it be your final hour.

Know, seventhly, of the Things thou art to expect in the commission of this Most Sacred Magick. Study the symbols well, and do not be afraid of any awful spectre that shall invade thine operation, or haunt thine habitat by day or by night. Only charge them with the words of the Covenant and they will do as you ask, if thou be strong. And if thou performest these operations often, thou shalt see things becoming dark; and the Wanderers in their Spheres shall no more be seen by thee; and the Stars in their places will lose their Light, and the Moon, NANNA, by whom thou also workest, shall become black and extinguished,

AND ARATAGAR SHALL BE NO MORE,
AND THE EARTH SHALL ABIDE NOT

And around thee shall appear the Flame, like Lightning, flashing in all directions, and all things will appear amid thunders, and from the Cavities of the Earth will leap forth the ANNUNNAKI, Dog-Faced, and thou shalt bring them down.

And the Sign of your Race is this:

Which thou shalt wear at all times, as the Sign of the Covenant between thee and the Elder Gods. And the Sign of the Elder Ones is this:

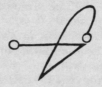

Which thou shalt wear at all times, as the sign of the Power of the Magick of ENKI. And I have told thee all this before, but I tell thee again, for the Priest, being furnished with every kind of Armor, and armed, he is similar to the Goddess.

The Place of Calling shall be high in the Mountains, most preferably; or near the Sea; or in some secluded area far from the thoughts of Man; or in the desert; or atop an ancient temple. And it shall be clean, and free from the unwanted. Thus, the Place, once chosen, shall be purified by supplications to thine particular God and Goddess, and by burning offerings of pine and cedar. And a round loaf shall be brought, and salt. And, having offered it to the personal deities, the Priest shall pronounce, solemnly, the following exorcism that the Place of Calling be cleansed and all Evil banished thereby; and the Priest shall not change one word or letter of this exorcism, but recite it faithfully as it is put down:

ENU SHUB
AM GIG ABSU
KISH EGIGGA
GAR SHAG DA SISIE AMARADA YA
DINGIR UD KALAMA SINIKU
DINGIR NINAB GUYU NEXRRANIKU
GA YA SHU SHAGMUKU TU!

And the Bread burned in the bronze brazier of Calling; and the Salt scattered about the room, sixty times.

And a Circle shall be drawn on the ground, in the midst whereof you shall stand while reciting the conjurations set forth, taking especial care not to venture forth from the boundaries of the Circle, the holy MANDAL of Calling, lest thou be consumed by the invisible monsters from the EGURRA of ERESHKIGAL, as was the Priest ABDUL BEN-MARTU in a public square in Jerusalem.

And the Circle shall be drawn in lime, or barley, or white flour. Or dug in the ground with the Dagger of INANNA of Calling. Or embroidered in the most precious silk, or expensive cloth.

And the colors thereof shall be only black and white, and no other.

And the Frontlet of Calling, and the Standards of Calling, shall all be of fine cloth, and in the colors of NINIB and INANNA, that is, of Black and White, for NINIB knows the Outer Regions and the ways of the Ancient Ones, and INANNA subdued the Underworld and vanquished the Queen thereof.

And the Crown of Calling shall bear the Eight-Rayed Star of the Elder Gods, and may be of beaten copper, set in with precious stones.

And thou shalt bear with thee a Rod of lapis lazuli, the Five-Rayed Star about thy neck, the Frontlet, the Girdle, the Amulet of UR about thine Arm, and a pure and unspotted Robe.

And these things shall be worn for the Operations of Calling only, and at other times shall be put away and hid, so that no eye may see them, save your own. As for the worship of the Gods, it is after the fashion of your country, but the Priests of Old were naked in their rites.

And thou shalt put down the Circle. And thou shalt invoke thy God and thy Goddess, but their Images must be removed from the altar and put away, unless thou call the Powers of MARDUK, in which case an Image of MARDUK should be set thereupon, and no other. And the perfumes must be burnt in the brazier after the Calling of the Fire, as set forth elsewhere in this Book. And the Watcher summoned, after Its fashion. And the Four Gates invoked, being the Four Watchtowers that stand about thee and the circumference of the MANDAL and witness the Rites, and Watch the Outside, that the Ancient Ones may not trouble thee.

And the Invocations of the Four Gates is after this fashion, which thou recite loudly, in a clear voice:

OF THE INVOCATION OF THE FOUR GATES FROM THE WORLD BETWEEN THE SPHERES

Invocation of the North Gate

Thee I invoke, Silver Hunter from the Sacred City of UR!

Thee I call forth to guard this North Place of the Most Holy Mandal against the vicious warriors of Flame from the Principalities of DRA!

Be thou most vigilant against the UTUKKI of TIAMAT

The Oppressors of ISHNIGARRAB

The Throne of AZAG-THOTH!

Draw Thy bow before the fiends of ABSU

Loose Thy arrow at the hordes of Dark Angels that beset the beloved of ARRA on all sides and in all places.

Be watchful, Lord of the North Ways.

Remember us, King of our Homeland, Victor of Every War and Conqueror over Every Adversary.

See our Lights and hear our Heralds, and do not forsake us.

Spirit of the North, Remember!

Invocation of the Eastern Gate

Thee I invoke, Mistress of the Rising Star,
Queen of Magick, of the Mountains of MASHU!
Thee I call forth this day to guard this Most Holy
mandal against the Seven Ensnarers, the Seven Liers-
In-Wait, the evil Maskim, the Evil Lords!
Thee I summon, Queen of the Eastern Ways, that thou
mayest protect me from the Eye of Death, and the
evil rays of the ENDUKUGGA and NINDUKUGGA!
Be watchful, Queen of the Eastern Ways, and
Remember!
Spirit of the East, Remember!

Invocation of the Southern Gate

Thee I invoke, Angel, Guardian against the URULU
Dread City of Death, Gate of No Return!
Do Thou stand at my side!
In the Names of the most Mighty Hosts of MARDUK and
ENKI, Lords of the Elder Race, the ARRA, do Thou
stand firm behind me!
Against PAZUZU and HUMWAWA, Fiends of the
Southwest Winds, do Thou stand firm!
Against the Lords of the Abominations, do Thou stand
firm!
Be Thou the Eyes behind me,
The Sword behind me,
The Spear behind me,
The Armour behind me.
Be watchful, Spirit of the Southern Ways, and
Remember!
Spirit of the South, Remember!

The Invocation of the Western Gate

Thee I invoke, Spirit of the Land of MER MARTU!
Thee I invoke, Angel of the Sunset!
From the Unknown God, protect me!
From the Unknown Demon, protect me!
From the Unknown Enemy, protect me!
From the Unknown Sorcery, protect me!
From the Waters of KUTULU, protect me!
From the Wrath of ERESHKIGAL, protect me!
From the Swords of KINGU, protect me!
From the Baneful Look, the Baneful Word, the Baneful
    Name, the Baneful Number, the Baneful Shape,
    protect me!
Be watchful, Spirit of the Western Ways, and Remember!

Spirit of the West Gate, Remember!

The Invocation of the Four Gates

MER SIDI!
MER KURRA!
MER URULU!
MER MARTU!
ZI DINGIR ANNA KANPA!
ZI DINGIR KIA KANPA!
UTUK XUL, TA ARDATA!
KUTULU, TA ATTALAKLA!
AZAG-THOTH, TA KALLA!
IA ANU! IA ENLIL! IA NNGI!
ZABAO!

Here follow several particular invocations, for summoning various Powers and Spirits. There may be Works of Necromantic Art, by which it is desirous to speak with the Phantom of someone dead, and perhaps dwelling in ABSU, and thereby a servant of ERESHKI-GAL, in which case the Preliminary Invocation that follows is to be used, which is the Invocation used by the Queen of Life, INANNA, at the time of her Descent into that Kingdom of Woe. It is no less than the Opening of the Gate of Ganzir, that leads to the Seven Steps into the frightful Pit. Therefore, do not be alarmed at the sights and sounds that will issue forth from that Opening, for they will be the wails and laments of the Shades that are chained therein, and the shrieking of the Mad God on the Throne of Darkness.

PRELIMINARY INVOCATION OF THE OPERATION OF CALLING OF THE SPIRITS OF THE DEAD WHO DWELL IN CUTHA, OF THE LOST.

BAAD ANGARRU!
NINNGHIZHIDDA!
Thee I invoke, Serpent of the Deep!
Thee I invoke, NINNGHIZHIDDA, Horned Serpent of the Deep!
Thee I invoke, Plumed Serpent of the Deep!
NINNGHIZHIDDA!
Open!
Open the Gate that I may enter!
NINNGHIZHIDDA, Spirit of the Deep, Watcher of the Gate, Remember!
In the Name of our Father, ENKI, before the Flight, Lord and Master of Magicians, Open the Gate that I may enter!

Open, lest I attack the Gate!

Open, lest I break down its bars!

Open, lest I attack the Walls!

Open, lest I leap over It by force!

Open the Gate, lest I cause the Dead to rise and devour the Living!

Open the Gate, lest I give the Dead power over the Living!

Open the Gate, lest I make the Dead to outnumber the Living!

NINNGHIZHIDDA, Spirit of the Deep, Watcher of the Gate, Open!

May the Dead rise and smell the incense!

And when the Spirit of the one called appears, do not be frightened at his Shape or condition, but say to him these words

UUG UDUUG UUGGA GISHTUGBI

and he will put on a comely appearance, and will answer truthfully all the questions you shall put to him, which he has wit to answer.

And it must be remembered that, after the questions have been answered to satisfaction, the Spirit is to be sent back to whence it came and not detained any longer, and no attempt must be made to free the Spirit, for that is in violation of the Covenant, and will bring upon thee and thy generations a most potent curse, wherefore it is unlawful to move the bones of the Dead or to disinter the bones of the Dead. And the Spirit may be sent back by means of these words

BARRA UUG UDUUG UUGGA!

and he will immediately disappear and return to his resting place. If he does not go at once, simply recite again those words, and he will do so.

The following is the Great Conjuration of All the Powers, to be used only in extreme necessity, or to silence a rebellious spirit who plagues thee, or who causeth consternation about the MANDAL for reasons unknown to thee, perhaps as agent for the Ancient Ones. In such a case, it is urgent to send back the Spirit before it gains in Power by dwelling in the Upper World, for as long as one of these is present upon the Earth, it gains in strength and Power until it is almost impossible to control them, as they are unto Gods.

This is the Conjuration, which thou recite forcefully:

THE GREAT CONJURATION OF ALL THE POWERS

SPIRIT OF THE SKY, REMEMBER!
SPIRIT OF THE EARTH, REMEMBER!

Spirits, Lords of the Earth, Remember!
Spirits, Ladies of the Earth, Remember!
Spirits, Lords of the Air, Remember!
Spirits, Ladies of the Air, Remember!
Spirits, Lords of the Fire, Remember!
Spirits, Ladies of the Fire, Remember!
Spirits, Lords of the Water, Remember!
Spirits, Ladies of the Water, Remember!
Spirits, Lords of the Stars, Remember!
Spirits, Ladies of the Stars, Remember!
Spirits, Lords of all hostilities, Remember!
Spirits, Ladies of all hostilities, Remember!
Spirits, Lords of all peacefulness, Remember!
Spirits, Ladies of all peacefulness, Remember!
Spirits, Lords of the Veil of Shadows, Remember!

Spirits, Ladies of the Veil of Shadows, Remember!
Spirits, Lords of the Light of Life, Remember!
Spirits, Ladies of the Light of Life, Remember!
Spirits, Lords of the Infernal Regions, Remember!
Spirits, Ladies of the Infernal Regions, Remember!
Spirits, Lords of the Lords of MARDUK, Remember!
Spirits, Ladies of the Ladies of MARDUK, Remember!
Spirits, Lords of SIN, Who maketh his ship cross the
    River, Remember!
Spirits, Ladies of SIN, Who maketh his ship cross the
    skies, Remember!
Spirits, Lords of SHAMMASH, King of the Elder Ones,
    Remember!
Spirits, Ladies of SHAMMASH GULA, Queen of the
    Elder Ones, Remember!
Spirits, Lords of TSHKU, Lord of the ANNUNAKI,
    Remember!
Spirits, Ladies of the Goddess ZIKU, Mother of ENKI,
    Remember!
Spirits, Lords of NINNASU, Our Father of the Numerous
    Waters, Remember!
Spirits, Ladies of NINNUAH, Daughter of ENKI,
    Remember!
Spirits, Lords of NINNGHIZHIDDA, Who upheaves the
    face of the Earth, Remember!
Spirits, Ladies of NINNISI ANA, Queen of Heaven,
    Remember!
Spirits, Lords and Ladies of the Fire, GIBIL, Ruler
    Supreme on the Face of the Earth, Remember!
Spirits of the Seven Doors of the World, Remember!
Spirits of the Seven Locks of the World, Remember!
Spirit KHUSBI KURU, Wife of NAMMTAR, Remember!

107

Spirit KHITIM KURUKU, Daughter of the Ocean,
    Remember!

SPIRIT OF THE SKY, REMEMBER!
SPIRIT OF THE EARTH, REMEMBER!

AMANU!
AMANU!
AMANU!

Here endeth the Great Conjuration.

THE CONJURATION OF IA ADU EN I
(A great Mystical Conjuration)

IA IA IA!
ADU EN I BA NINIB
NINIB BA FIRIK
FIRIK BA PIRIK
PIRIK BA AGGA BA ES
AGGA BA ES BA AKKA BAR!
AKKA BAR BA AKKA BA ES
AKKA BA ES BA AKKA BAR
AKKA BAR BA AGGA BA ES
AGGA BA ES BA PIRIK
PIRIK BA FIRIK
FIRIK BA NINIB
NINIB BA ADU EN I
IAIAIAIA!
KUR BUR IA!
EDIN BA EGA

ERIM BA EGURA
E! E! E!
IA IA IA!
EKHI IAK SAKKAK
EKHI AZAG-THOTH
EKHI ASARU
EKHI CUTHALU
IA! IA! IA!

WHAT SPIRITS MAY BE USEFUL

In the Ceremonies of Calling, any type of Spirit may be summoned and detained until It has answered your questions or provided you with whatever you desire. The Spirits of the Dead may be invoked. The Spirits of the Unborn may be invoked. The Spirits of the Seven Spheres may be invoked. The Spirits of the Flame may be invoked. In all, there may be One Thousand-and-One Spirits that are of principal importance, and these you will come to know in the course of your experiments. There are many others, but some have no power, and will only confuse.

The best Spirits to summon in the early Rites are the Fifty Spirits of the Names of Lord MARDUK, who give excellent attendance and who are careful Watchers of the Outside. They should not be detained any longer than is necessary, and some are indeed of violent and impatient natures, and their task is to be given in as short a time as possible, and then they are to be released.

After these, the Spirits of the seven Spheres may be invoked to advantage, after the Priest has already trod their Ways after the manner of the Walking.

After the Priest has gained Entrance to the Gate of NANNA, he may summon the Spirits of that Realm, but not before. These things you will learn in the course of your journey, and it is not necessary to put it all down here, save for a few noble formulae concerning the Works of the Sphere of LIBAT, of ISHTAR, the Queen.

These are Works of the gentle passions, which seek to engender affection between man and woman. And they may best be done in a Circle of white, the Priest being properly cleansed and in a clean robe.

Preliminary Purfication Invocation

Bright One of the Heavens, wise ISHTAR
Mistress of the Gods, whose "yes" is truly "yes"
Proud One among the Gods, whose command is supreme
Mistress of Heaven and of Earth, who rules in all places
ISHTAR, at your Name all heads are bowed down
I ... son of ... have bowed down before you
May my body be purified like lapis lazuli!
May my face be bright like alabaster!
Like shining silver and reddish gold may I not be dull!

To Win the Love of a Woman

(chant the following three times over an apple or a pomegranate; give the fruit to the woman to drink of the juices, and she will surely come to you.)

MUNUS SIGSIGGA AG BARA YE
INNIN AGGISH XASHXUR GISHNU URMA
SHAZIGA BARA YE
ZIGASHUBBA NA AGSISHAMAZIGA
NAMZA YE INNIN DURRE ESH AKKI
UGU AGBA ANDAGUB!

To Recover Potency

(Tie three knots in a harp string; entwine around both right and left hands, and chant the following incantation seven times, and potency will return.)

LILLIK IM LINU USH KIRI
LISHTAKSSIR ERPETUMMA TIKU LITTUK
NI YISH LIBBI IA LU AMESH ID GINMESH
ISHARI LU SAYAN SAYAMMI YE
LA URRADA ULTU MUXXISHA!

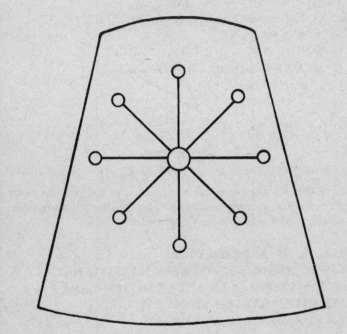

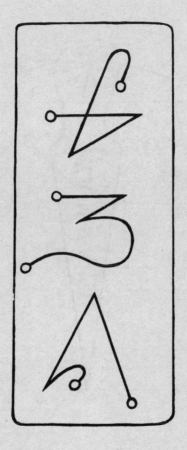

THE COPPER DAGGER OF INANNA OF CALLING

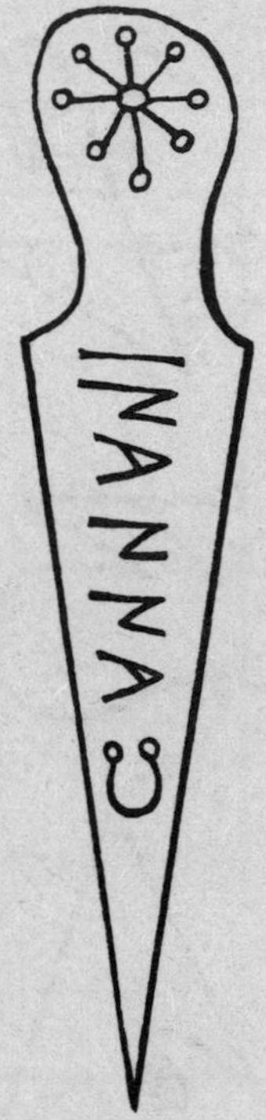

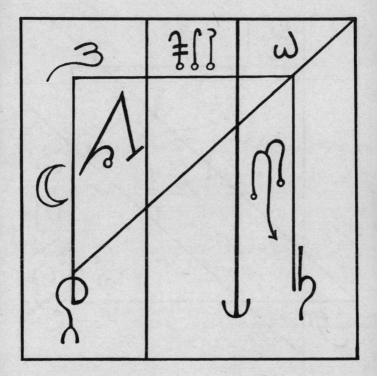

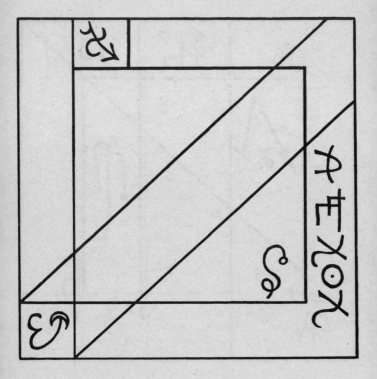

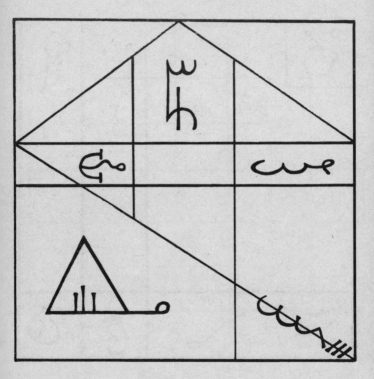

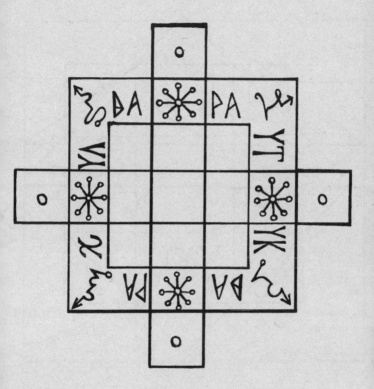

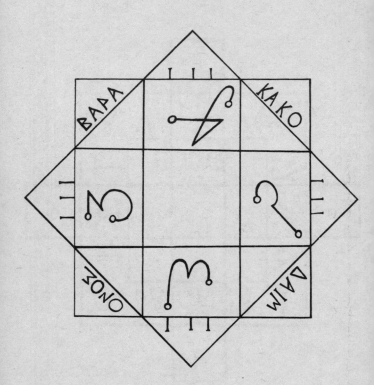

The

Book

of

Fifty

Names

THE BOOK OF THE FIFTY NAMES OF MARDUK, DEFEATER OF THE ANCIENT ONES

THIS is the Book of MARDUK, begotten of our Master ENKI, Lord of Magicians, who did defeat TIAMAT, known as KUR, known as HUWAWA, in magick combat, who defeated the Ancient Ones that the Elders may live and rule the Earth.

In the time before time, in the age before the heaven and the earth were put in their places, in the age when the Ancient Ones were rulers of all that existed and did not exist, there was nought but darkness. There was no Moon. There was no Sun. No planets were they, and no stars. No grain, no tree, no plant grew. The Ancient Ones were Masters of Spaces now unknown or forgotten, and all was CHAOS.

MARDUK was chosen of the Elders to fight KUR and wrest power from the Great Sleeping Serpent who dwells beneath the Mountains of the Scorpion. MARDUK was given a weapon, and a Sign, and Fifty Powers were given to him to fight the awful TIAMAT, and each Power has its weapon and its Sign and these are the mightiest possessions of the Elder Gods against the Ancient One who threatens from Without, who threatens from the Abyss, the Lord of Darkness, the Master of CHAOS, the Unborn, the Uncreated, who still wishes ill upon the Race of Men, and upon the Elder Gods who reside in the Stars.

The Gods forget. They are distant. They must be reminded. If they are not watchful, if the gatekeepers do not watch the gates, if the gates are not kept always locked, bolted and barred, then the One who is always ready, the Guardian of the Other side, IAK SAKKAK, will enter and bring with him the hordes of the armies of the Ancient Ones, IAK KINGU, IAK AZAG, IAK AZABUA, IAK HUWAWA, ISHNIGGARAB, IAK XASTUR, and IAK KUTULU, the Dog Gods and the Dragon Gods, and the Sea Monsters, and the Gods of the Deep.

Watch also the Days. The Day when the Great Bear hangs lowest in the sky, and the quarters of the year measured thereof in the four directions measured thereof, for there the Gates may be opened and care must needs be taken to ensure that the Gates remain forever closed. They must be sealed with the Elder Sign, accompanied by the rites and incantations proper.

The Fifty Names here follow, with their Signs and Powers. They may be summoned after the Priest has ascended to that step on the Ladder of Lights and gained entrance to that Sacred City. The Signs should be engraved on parchment or sealed in clay and placed upon the altar at the Calling. And the perfumes should be of cedar, and strong, sweet-smelling resins. And the Calling be to the North.

The First Name is MARDUK

The Lord of Lords, Master of Magicians. His Name should not be called except when no other will do , and it is the most terrible responsibility to do so. The Word of His Calling is DUGGA.
This is his Seal:

The Second Name is MARUKKA

Knows all things since the beginning of the World. Knows all secrets, be they human or divine, and is very difficult to summon. The Priest should not summon him unless he is clean of heart and spirit, for this Spirit shall know his innermost thoughts.
This is his Seal:

The Third Name is MARUTUKKU

Master of the Arts of Protection, chained the
Mad God at the Battle. Sealed the Ancient Ones in their
Caves, behind the Gates. Possesses the ARRA star. This
is his Seal:

The Fourth Name is BARASHAKUSHU

Worker of Miracles. The kindest of the Fifty, and
the most beneficent. The Word used at his Calling is
BAALDURU. This is his Seal:

The Fifth Name is LUGGALDIMMERANKIA

Put order into CHAOS. Made the Waters aright. Commander of Legions of Wind Demons who fought the Ancient TIAMAT alongside MARDUK KURIOS. The Word used at his Calling is BANUTUKKU. This is his Seal:

The Sixth Name is NARILUGGALDIMMERANKIA

The Watcher of the IGIGI and the ANNUNAKI, Sub-Commander of the Wind Demons. He will put to flight any maskim who haunt thee, and is the foe of the rabisu. None may pass into the World Above or the World Below without his knowledge. His Word is BANRABI-SHU. His Seal is thus:

The Seventh Name is ASARULUDU

Wielder of the Flaming Sword, oversees the Race of Watchers at the bidding of the Elder Gods. He ensures the most perfect safety, especially in dangerous tasks undertaken at the behest of the Astral Gods. His word is BANMASKIM and his Seal is thus:

The Eighth Name is NAMTILLAKU

A most secret and potent Lord, he hath knowledge to raise the dead and converse with the spirits of the Abyss, unbeknownst to their Queen. No soul passes into Death but that he is aware. His Word is BANUTUKUKUTUKKU and his Seal is thus:

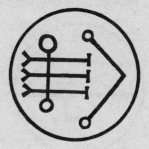

The Ninth Name is NAMRU

Dispenses wisdom and knowledge in all things. Giveth excellent counsel and teaches the science of metals. His Word is BAKAKALAMU and his Seal:

The Tenth Name is ASARU

This Power has knowledge of all plants and trees, and can make marvellous fruits to grow in the desert places, and no land is a waste to him. He is truly the Protector of the Bounty. His Word is BAALPRIKU and his Seal follows:

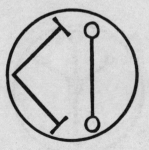

The Eleventh Name is ASARUALIM

Possesses secret wisdom, and shines Light in the Darkened areas, forcing what lives there to give good accounting of its existence and its knowledge. Giveth excellent counsel in all things. His Word is BARRMARA-TU and the Seal which thou engrave is thus:

The Twelfth Name is ASARUALIMNUNNA

This is the Power that presideth over armor of all kinds and is excellently knowledgeable in military matters, being of the advance army of MARDUK at that Battle. He can provide an army with its entire weaponry in three days. His Word is BANATATU and the Seal is thus:

The Thirteenth Name is TUTU

Silences the weeping and gives joy to the sad and ill at heart. A most beneficent Name, and Protector of the Household, his Word is DIRRIGUGIM and his Seal is this:

The Fourteenth Name is ZIUKKINNA

Giveth excellent knowledge concerning the movements of the stars and the meanings thereof, of which the Chaldaens possessed this same knowledge in abundance. The Word is GIBBILANNU and the Seal is this:

The Fifteenth Name is ZIKU

This Power bestoweth Riches of all kinds, and can tell where treasury is hidden. Knower of the Secrets of the Earth. His Word is GIGGIMAGANPA and his Seal is this:

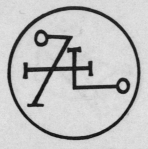

The Sixteenth Name is AGAKU

This Power can give life to what is already dead, but for a short time only. He is the Lord of the Amulet and the Talisman. His Word is MASHGARZANNA and his Seal is this:

The Seventeenth Name is TUKU

Lord of Baneful Magick, Vanquisher of the Ancient Ones by Magick, Giver of the Spell to MARDUK KUROS, a most fierce enemy. His Word is MASH-SHAMMASHTI and his Seal follows:

The Eighteenth Name is SHAZU

Knows the thoughts of those at a distance, as well as those in the vicinity. Nothing is buried in the ground, or thrown into the water, but this Power is aware. His Word is MASHSHANANNA and his Seal is this:

The Nineteenth Name is ZISI

Reconciler of enemies, silencer of arguments, between two people or between two nations, or even, it is said, between two worlds. The scent of Peace is indeed sweet to this Power, whose Word is MASHINANNA and whose seal is this:

The Twentieth Name is SUHRIM

Seeks out the worshippers of the Ancient Ones wherever they may be. The Priest who sends him on an errand does so at a terrible risk, for SUHRIM kills easily, and without thought. His Word is MASHSHANERGAL and his Seal:

The Twenty-First Name is SUHGURIM

As SUHRIM above, the Foe who Cannot be Appeased. Discovers the Priest's Enemies with ease, but must be cautioned not to slay them if the Priest does not desire it. The Word is MASHSHADAR and the Seal:

The Twenty-Second Name is ZAHRIM

Slew ten thousand of the Hordes in the Battle. A Warrior among Warriors. Can destroy an entire army if the Priest so desires. His Word is MASHSHAGARANNU and his Seal:

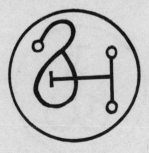

The Twenty-Third Name is ZAHGURIM

As ZAHRIM, a most terrible opponent. It is said ZAHGURIM slays slowly, after a most unnatural fashion. I do not know, for I have never summoned this Spirit. It is thy risk. The Word is MASHTISHADDU and the Seal:

The Twenty-Fourth Name is ENBILULU

This Power can seek out water in the midst of a desert or on the tops of mountains. Knows the Secrets of Water, and the running of rivers below the Earth. A most useful Spirit. His Word is MASHSHANEBBU and his Seal thus:

The Twenty-Fifth Name is EPADUN

This is the Lord of all Irrigation and can bring Water from a far place to your feet. Possesses a most subtle geometry of the Earth and knowledge of all lands where Water might be found in abundance. His Word is EYUNGINAKANPA and his Seal is this:

The Twenty-Sixth Name is ENBILULUGUGAL

The Power that presides over all growth, and all that grows. Gives knowledge of cultivation, and can supply a starving city with food for thirteen moons in one moon. A most noble Power. His Word is AGGHA and his Seal:

The Twenty-Seventh Name is HEGAL

As the Power above, a Master of the arts of farming and agriculture. Bestows rich harvests. Possesses the knowledge of the metals of the earth, and of the plough. His Word is BURDISHU and his seal thus:

The Twenty-Eighth Name is SIRSIR

The Destroyer of TIAMAT, hated of the Ancient Ones, Master over the Serpent, Foe of KUTULU. A most powerful Lord. His Word is this APIRIKUBABADAZU-ZUKANPA and his Seal:

The Twenty-Ninth Name is MALAH

Trod the back of the Worm and cut it in twain. Lord of Bravery and Courage, and gives these qualities to the Priest who desires it, or to others the Priest may decide. The Word is BACHACHADUGGA and the Seal:

The Thirtieth Name is GIL

The Furnisher of Seed. Beloved of ISHTAR, his Power is mysterious and quite ancient. Makes the barley to grow and the women to give birth. Makes potent the impotent. His Word is AGGABAL and his Seal is thus:

The Thirty-First Name is GILMA

Founder of cities, Possessor of the Knowledge of Architecture by which the fabled temples of UR were built; the creator of all that is permanent and never moves. His Word is AKKABAL and his Seal is this:

The Thirty-Second Name is AGILMA

Bringer of Rain. Maketh the gentle Rains to come, or causeth great Storms and Thunders, the like may destroy armies and cities and crops. His Word is MASHSHAYEGURRA and his Seal is:

The Thirty-Third Name is ZULUM

Knows where to plant and when to plant. Giveth excellent counsel in all manner of business and commerce. Protects a man from evil tradesmen. His Word is ABBABAAL and his Seal is this:

The Thirty-Fourth Name is MUMMU

The Power given to MARDUK to fashion the universe from the flesh of TIAMAT. Giveth wisdom concerning the condition of life before the creation, and the nature of the structures of the Four Pillars whereupon the Heavens rest. His Word is ALALALA-BAAAL and the Seal is:

The Thirty-Fifth Name is ZULUMMAR

Giveth tremendous strength, as of ten men, to one man. Lifted the part of TIAMAT that was to become the Sky from the part that was to become the Earth. His Word is ANNDARABAAL and his Seal is:

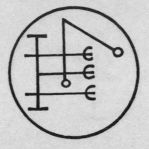

The Thirty-Sixth Name is LUGALABDUBUR

Destroyer of the Gods of TIAMAT. Vanquisher of Her Hordes. Chained KUTULU to the Abyss. Fought AZAG-THOTH with skill. A great Defender and a great Attacker. His Word is AGNIBAAL and his Seal is this:

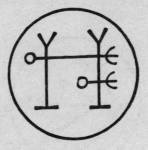

The Thirty-Seventh Name is PAGALGUENNA

Possessor of Infinite Intelligence, and determines the nature of things not yet made, and of spirits not yet created, and knows the strength of the Gods. His Word is ARRABABAAL and his Seal is this:

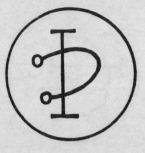

The Thirty-Eighth Name is LUGALDURMAH

The Lord of the Lofty Places, Watcher of the Skies and all that travels therein. Naught traverses the starry element, but that this Power is aware. His Word is ARATAAGARBAL and his Seal is this:

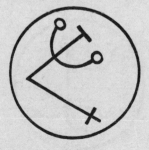

The Thirty-Ninth Name is ARANUNNA

Giver of Wisdom, Counselor to our Father, ENKI, Knower of the Magickal Covenant and of the Laws and of the Nature of the Gates. His Word is ARAMANNGI and his Seal is thusly:

The Fortieth Name is DUMUDUKU

Possessor of the Wand of Lapis Lazuli, Knower of the Secret Name and the Secret Number. May not reveal these to thee, but may speak of other things, equally marvelous. His Word is ARATAGIGI and his Seal is:

The Forty-First Name is LUGALANNA

The Power of the Eldest of the Elder Ones, possesses the secret knowledge of the world when the Ancient Ones and the Elder Ones were One. Knows the Essence of the Ancient Ones and where it might be found. His Word is BALDIKHU and his Seal is this:

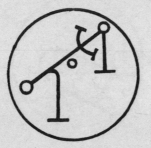

The Forty-Second Name is LUGALUGGA

Knows the Essences of all Spirits, of the Dead and the Unborn, and the Starry and the Earthly, and the Spirits of the Air and the Spirits of the Wind as well. Which things he may tell thee, and thou wilt grow in wisdom. His Word is ZIDUR and his Seal is thus:

The Forty-Third Name is IRKINGU

This is the Power that laid capture to the Commander of the forces of the Ancient Ones, KINGU, Mighty Demon, that MARDUK might lay hold of him and, with its blood, create the Race of Men and seal the Covenant. His Word is BARERIMU and his Seal is this:

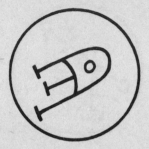

The Forty-Fourth Name is KINMA

Judge and Lord of the Gods, at whose name they quake in fear. That the Gods may not err, this Power was given to oversee their activities, should they be lawful and within the nature of the Covenant, for the Gods are forgetful, and very far away. His Word is ENGAIGAI and his Seal is this:

The Forty-Fifth Name is ESIZKUR

This Spirit possesses the knowledge of the length of Life of any man, even unto the plants and the demons and the gods. He measureth all things, and knoweth the Space thereof. His Word is NENIGEGAI and his Seal is this:

The Forty-Sixth Name is GIBIL

This Power has been given the Realm of the Fire and the Forge. He keepeth the sharp point of the Sword and the Lance, and giveth understanding in the working of metals. He also raises the Lightning that comes from the Earth, and maketh Swords to appear in the Sky. His Word is BAALAGNITARRA and his Seal is this:

The Forty-Seventh Name is ADDU

Raises storms that fill the entire heavens and causes the Stars to tremble and the very Gates of the IGIGI to shake in their stead. Can fill the skies with his brightness, even in the darkest hour of the night. His Word is KAKODAMMU and his Seal is this:

The Forty-Eighth Name is ASHARRU

Knower of the Treacherous Ways. Gives intelligence of the Future and also of things Past. Put the Gods in their courses, and determined their cycles. His Word is BAXTANDABAL and this is his Seal:

The Forty-Ninth Name is NEBIRU

The Spirit of the Gate of MARDUK. Manages all things in their ways, and moves the crossings of the stars after the fashion known to the Chaldeans. His word is DIRGIRGIRI and his Seal is this:

The Fiftieth Name is NINNUAM

This is the Power of MARDUK as Lord of All That Is, Judger of Judgements, Decider of Decisions, He Who Determines the Laws and the Reigns of Kings. He may not be called, save at the destruction of a city or the death of a king. His Word is GASHDIG and his Seal is this:

Here endeth the Book of the Fifty Names, which the Gods have granted me the strength and the time in which to lay it down. This Book is not to be shown to the unclean or the profane or the uninitiated, for to do so is to call the most awful curse of the Book upon thee and upon thy generations.

Spirit of the Book, Remember!

The

MAGAN

Text

HE verses here following come from the secret text of some of the priests of a cult which is all that is left of the Old Faith that existed before Babylon was built, and it was originally in their tongue, but I have put it into the Golden Speech of my country so that you may understand it. I came upon this text in my early wanderings in the region of the Seven Fabled Cities of UR, which are no more, and it tells of the War between the Gods that took place in a time beyond the memory of Man. And the horrors and ugliness that the Priest will encounter in his Rites are herein described, and their reasons, and their natures, and Essences. And the Number of the Lines is Sacred, and the Words are Sacred, and are most potent charms against the Evil Ones. And surely some Magicians of the country do write them on parchment or clay, or on pottery, or in the air, that they might be efficacious thereby, and that the Gods will remember the words of the Covenant.

I copied these words down in my tongue and kept them faithfully these many years, and my own copy will go with me to the place where I will go when my Spirit is torn from my body. But heed these words well, and remember! For remembering is the most important and most potent magick, being the Rememberance of Things Past and the Rememberance of Things to Come, which is the same Memory. And do not show this text to the uninitiated, for it hath caused madness, in men and in beasts.

The Text:

Hearken, and Remember!
In the Name of ANU, Remember!
In the Name of ENLIL, Remember!
In the Name of ENKI, Remember!
When on High the Heavens had not been named,
The Earth had not been named,
And Naught existed but the Seas of ABSU,
The Ancient One,
And MUMMU TIAMAT, the Ancient One
Who bore them all,
Their Waters as One Water.
At this time, before the ELDER GODS had been brought
    forth,
Uncalled by Name,
Their destinies unknown and undetermined,
Then it was that the Gods were formed within the
    Ancient Ones.
LLMU and LLAAMU were brought forth and called by
    Name,
And for Ages they grew in age and bearing.
ANSHAR and KISHAR were brought forth,
And brought forth ANU
Who begat NUDIMMUD, Our Master ENKI,
Who has no rival among the Gods.
Remember!
The Elder Ones came together
They disturbed TIAMAT, the Ancient One, as they surged
    back and forth.
Yea, they troubled the belly of TIAMAT
By their Rebellion in the abode of Heaven.

ABSU could not lessen their clamor
TIAMAT was speechless at their ways.
Their doings were loathsome unto the Ancient Ones.

ABSU rose up to slay the Elder Gods by stealth.
With magick charm and spell ABSU fought,
But was slain by the sorcery of the Elder Gods.
And it was their first victory.
His body was lain in an empty Space
In a crevice of the heavens
Hid
He was lain,
But his blood cried out to the Abode of Heaven.

TIAMAT
Enraged
Filled with an Evil Motion
Said
Let us make Monsters
That they may go out and do battle
Against these Sons of Iniquity
The murderous offspring who have destroyed
A God.
HUBUR arose, She who fashioneth all things,
And possessor of Magick like unto Our Master.
She added matchless weapons to the arsenals of the
    Ancient Ones,
She bore Monster-Serpents
Sharp of tooth, long of fang,
She filled their bodies with venom for blood
Roaring dragons she has clothed with Terror
Has crowned them with Halos, making them as Gods,

So that he who beholds them shall perish
And, that, with their bodies reared up
None might turn them back.
She summoned the Viper, the Dragon, and the Winged
     Bull,
The Great Lion, the Mad-Dog, and the Scorpion-Man.
Mighty rabid Demons, Feathered-Serpents, the Horse-
     Man,
Bearing weapons that spare not
Fearless in Battle,
Charmed with the spells of ancient sorcery,
...withal Eleven of this kind she brought forth
With KINGU as Leader of the Minions.

Remember!

ENKI
Our Master
Fearing defeat, summoned his Son
MARDUK
Summoned his Son
The Son of Magick
Told him the Secret Name
The Secret Number
The Secret Shape
Whereby he might do battle
With the Ancient Horde
And be victorious.

MARDUK KURIOS!
Brightest Star among the Stars
Strongest God among the Gods

Son of Magick and the Sword
Child of Wisdom and the Word
Knower of the Secret Name
Knower of the Secret Number
Knower of the Secret Shape
He armed himself with the Disc of Power
In chariots of Fire he went forth
With a shouting Voice he called the Spell
With a Blazing Flame he filled his Body
Dragons, Vipers, all fell down
Lions, Horse-Men, all were slain.
The Mighty Creatures of HUBUR were slain
The Spells, the Charms, the Sorcery were broken.
Naught but TIAMAT remained.
The Great Serpent, the Enormous Worm
The Snake with iron teeth
The Snake with sharpened claw
The Snake with Eyes of Death,
She lunged at MARDUK
With a roar
With a curse
She lunged.
MARDUK struck with the Disc of Power
Blinded TIAMAT's Eyes of Death
The Monster heaved and raised its back
Struck forth in all directions
Spitting ancient words of Power
Screamed the ancient incantations
MARDUK struck again and blew
An Evil Wind into her body
Which filled the raging, wicked Serpent
MARDUK shot between her jaws

The Charmed arrow of ENKI's Magick
MARDUK struck again and severed
The head of TIAMAT from its body.

And all was silent.

Remember!

MARDUK
Victor
Took the Tablets of Destiny
Unbidden
Hung them around his neck.
Acclaimed of the Elder Gods was he.
First among the Elder Ones was he.
He split the sundered TIAMAT in twain
And fashioned the heavens and the earth,
With a Gate to keep the Ancient Ones Without.
With a Gate whose Key is hid forever
Save to the Sons of MARDUK
Save to the Followers of Our Master
ENKI
First in Magick among the Gods.

From the Blood of KINGU he fashioned Man.
He constructed Watchtowers for the Elder Gods
Fixing their astral bodies as constellations
That they may watch the Gate of ABSU
The Gate of TIAMAT they watch
The Gate of KINGU they oversee
The Gate whose Guardian is IAK SAKKAK they bind.

All the Elder Powers resist
The Force of Ancient Artistry
The Magick Spell of the Oldest Ones
The Incantation of the Primal Power
The Mountain KUR, the Serpent God
The Mountain MASHU, that of Magick
The Dead KUTULU, Dead but Dreaming
TIAMAT, Dead but Dreaming
ABSU, KINGU, Dead but Dreaming
And shall their generation come again?

WE ARE THE LOST ONES
From a Time before Time
From a Land beyond the Stars
From the Age when ANU walked the earth
In company of Bright Angels.
We have survived the first War
Between the Powers of the Gods
And have seen the wrath of the Ancient Ones
Dark Angels
Vent upon the Earth
WE ARE FROM A RACE BEYOND THE WANDERERS
    OF NIGHT.
We have survived the Age when ABSU ruled the Earth
And the Power destroyed our generations.
We have survived on tops of mountains
And beneath the feet of mountains
And have spoken with the Scorpions
In allegiance and were betrayed.
And TIAMAT has promised us nevermore to attack
With water and with wind.
But the Gods are forgetful.

Beneath the Seas of NAR MATTARU
Beneath the Seas of the Earth, NAR MATTARU
Beneath the World lays sleeping
The God of Anger, Dead but Dreaming
The God CUTHALU, Dead but Dreaming!
The Lord of KUR, calm but thunderous!
The One-Eyed Sword, cold but burning!

He who awakens Him calls the ancient
Vengeance of the Elder Ones
The Seven Glorious Gods
Of the Seven Glorious Cities
Upon himself and upon the World
An old vengeance...

Know that our years are the years of War
And our days are measured as battles
And every hour is a Life
Lost to the Outside
Those from Without
Have builded up charnel houses
To nourish the fiends of TIAMAT
And the Blood of the weakest here
Is libation unto TIAMAT
Queen of the Ghouls
Wreaker of Pain
And to invoke her
The Red Water of Life
Need be spilt on a stone
The stone struck with a sword
That hath slain eleven men
Sacrifices to HUBUR

So that the strike ringeth out
And call TIAMAT from Her slumber
From her sleep in the Caverns
Of the Earth.

And none may dare entreat further
For to invoke Death is to utter
The final prayer.

II
Of The Generations of the Ancient Ones

UTUKK XUL
The accounts of the generations
Of the Ancient Ones here rendered
Of the generations of the Ancient Ones
Here remembered.
Cold and Rain that erode all things
They are the Evil Spirits
In the creation of ANU spawned
Plague Gods
PAZUZU
And the Beloved Sons of ENG
The Offspring of NINNKIGAL
Rending in pieces on high
Bringing destruction below
They are the Children of the Underworld
Loudly roaring on high
Gibbering loathsomely below
They are the bitter venom of the Gods.
The great storms directed from heaven
Those are they

The Owl, Messenger of UGGI
Lord of Death
Those they are
THEY ARE THE CHILDREN
BORN OF EARTH
THAT IN THE CREATION
OF ANU WERE SPAWNED.

The highest walls
The thickest walls
The strongest walls
Like a flood they pass
From house to house
They ravage
No door can shut them out
No bolt can turn them back
Through the door like snakes they slide
Through the bolts like winds they blow
Pulling the wife from the embrace of the husband
Snatching the child from the loins of man
Banishing the man from his home, his land
THEY ARE THE BURNING PAIN
THAT PRESSETH ITSELF ON THE BACK OF MAN.

THEY ARE THE GHOULS
The spirit of the harlot that hath died in the streets
The spirit of the woman that hath died in childbirth
The spirit of the woman that hath died, weeping with a
    babe at the breast
The spirit of an evil man
One that haunteth the streets
Or one that haunteth the bed.

They are Seven!
Seven are they!
Those Seven were born in the Mountains of MASHU
Called Magick
They dwell within the Caverns of the Earth
Amid the desolate places of the Earth they live
Amid the places between
The Places
Unknown in heaven and in earth
They are arrayed in terror
Among the Elder Gods there is no knowledge of them
They have no name
Not in heaven
Nor on earth
They ride over the Mountain of Sunset
And on the Mountain of Dawn they cry
Through the Caverns of the Earth they creep
Amid the desolate places of the Earth they lie
Nowhere are they known
Not in heaven
Nor in the Earth
Are they discovered
For their place is outside our place
And between the angles of the Earth
They lie in wait
Crouching for the Sacrifice
THEY ARE THE CHILDREN OF THE UNDERWORLD.

Falling like rain from the sky
Issuing like mist from the earth
Doors do not stop them
Bolts do not stop them

They glide in at the doors like serpents
They enter by the windows like the wind
IDPA they are, entering by the head
NAMTAR they are, entering by the heart
UTUK they are, entering by the brow
ALAL they are, entering by the chest
GIGIM they are, seizing the bowels
TELAL they are, grasping the hand
URUKU they are, giant Larvae, feeding on the Blood
They are Seven!
Seven are They!
They seize all the towers
From UR to NIPPUR
Yet UR knows them not
Yet NIPPUR does not know them
They have brought down the mighty
Of all the mighty Cities of man
Yet man knows them not
Yet the Cities do not know them
They have struck down the forests of the East
And have flooded the Lands of the West
Yet the East knows them not
Yet the West does not know them
They are a hand grasping at the neck
Yet the neck does not know them
And man knows them not.
Their words are Unwrit
Their numbers are Unknown
Their shapes are all Shapes
Their habitations
The desolate places where their Rites are performed
Their habitations

The haunts of man where a sacrifice has been offered
Their habitations
The lands here
The cities here
And the lands between the lands
The cities between the cities
In spaces no man has ever walked
In KURNUDE
The country from whence no traveler returns
At EKURBAD
In the altar of the Temple of the Dead
And at GI UMUNA
At their Mother's breast
At the Foundations of CHAOS
In the ARALIYA of MUMMU-TIAMAT
And at the Gates
Of IAK SAKKAK!

SPIRIT OF THE AIR, REMEMBER!
SPIRIT OF THE EARTH, REMEMBER!

III

Of the Forgotten Generations of Man

And was not Man created from the blood of KINGU
Commander of the hordes of the Ancient Ones?
Does not man possess in his spirit
The seed of rebellion against the Elder Gods?
And the blood of Man is the Blood of Vengeance
And the blood of Man is the Spirit of Vengeance

And the Power of Man is the Power of the Ancient Ones
And this is the Covenant
For, lo! The Elder Gods possess the Sign
By which the Powers of the Ancient Ones are turned back
But Man possesses the Sign
And the Number
And the Shape
To summon the Blood of his Parents.
And this is the Covenant.
Created by the Elder Gods
From the Blood of the Ancient Ones
Man is the Key by which
The Gate of IAK SAKKAK may be flung wide
By which the Ancient Ones
Seek their Vengeance
Upon the face of the Earth
Against the Offspring of MARDUK.
For what is new
Came from that which is old
And what is old
Shall replace that which is new
And once again the Ancient Ones
Shall rule upon the face of the Earth!
And this is too the Covenant!

IV

Of the Sleep of ISHTAR

Yet ISHTAR
Queen of Heaven
Bright Light of Nights

Mistress of the Gods
Set her mind in that direction
From Above she set her mind,
To Below she set her mind
From the Heavens she set forth
To the Abyss
Out of the Gates of the Living
To enter the Gates of Death
Out of the Lands we know
Into the Lands we know not
To the Land of No Return
To the Land of Queen ERESHKIGAL
ISHTAR, Queen of Heavens, she set her mind
ISHTAR, Daughter of SIN, she set forth
To the Black Earth, the Land of CUTHA
She set forth
To the House of No Return she set her foot
Upon the Road whence None Return
She set her foot
To the Cave, forever unlit
Where bowls of clay are heaped upon the altar
Where bowls of dust are the food
Of residents clothed only in wings
To ABSU ISHTAR set forth.
Where sleeps the dread CUTHALU
ISHTAR set forth.

The Watcher
Stood fast.
The Watcher
NINNGHIZHIDDA
Stood fast.

And ISHTAR spoke unto him

NINNGHIZHIDDA! Serpent of the Deep!
NINNGHIZHIDDA! Horned Serpent of the Deep!
NINNGHIZHIDDA! Plumed Serpent of the Deep!
Open!
Open the Door that I may enter!
NINNGHIZHIDDA, Spirit of the Deep, Watcher of the
     Gate, Remember!
In the Name of our Father before the Flight, ENKI, Lord
     and Master of Magicians
Open the Door that I may enter!
Open
Lest I attack the Door
Lest I break apart its bars
Lest I attack the Barrier
Lest I take its walls by force
Open the Door
Open Wide the Gate
Lest I cause the Dead to rise!
I will raise up the Dead!
I will cause the Dead to rise and devour the living!
Open the Door
Lest I cause the Dead to outnumber the Living!
NINNGHIZHIDDA, Spirit of the Deep, Watcher of the
     Gate, Open!

NINNGHIZHIDDA
The Great Serpent
Coiled back on itself
And answered
ISHTAR

Lady
Queen among the Gods
I go before my Mistress
ERESHKIGAL
Before the Queen of Death
I will announce Thee.

And NINNGHIZHIDDA
Horned Serpent
Approached the Lady ERESHKIGAL
And said:
Behold, ISHTAR, Thy Sister
Queen among the Gods
Stands before the Gate!
Daughter of SIN, Mistress of ENKI
She waits.

And ERESHKIGAL was pale with fear.
The Dark Waters stirred.

Go, Watcher of the Gate.
Go, NINNGHIZHIDDA, Watcher of the Gate,
Open the Door to ISHTAR
And treat Her as it is written
In the Ancient Covenant.

And NINNGHIZHIDDA loosed the bolt from the hatch
And Darkness fell upon ISHTAR
The Dark Waters rose and carried the Goddess of Light
To the Realms of the Night.
And the Serpent spoke:
Enter

Queen of Heaven of the Great Above
That KUR may rejoice
That CUTHA may give praise
That KUTU may smile.
Enter
That KUTULU may be pleased at Thy presence.

And ISHTAR entered.

And there are Seven Gates and Seven Decrees.

At the First Gate
    NINNGHIZHIDDA removed the Crown
    The Great Crown of Her head he took away
    And ISHTAR asked
    Why, Serpent, has thou removed my First Jewel?
    And the Serpent answered
    Thus it is, the Covenant of Old, set down before
    Time,
    The Rules of the Lady of KUTU.
    Enter the First Gate.

At the Second Gate
    NINNGHIZHIDDA removed the Wand
    The Wand of Lapis Lazuli he took away
    And ISHTAR asked
    Why, NETI, hast thou removed my Second Jewel?
    And NETI answered
    Thus it is, the Covenant of Old, set down before
        Time
    The Decrees of the Lady of KUTU.
    Enter the Second Gate.

At the Third Gate

NINNGHIZHIDDA removed the Jewels

The Jewels around her neck he took away

And ISHTAR asked

Why, Gatekeeper, has thou removed my Third
Jewel?

And the Gatekeeper answered

Thus it is, the Covenant of Old, set down before
Time,

The Decrees of the Lady of KUTU

Enter the Third Gate.

At the Fourth Gate

NINNGHIZHIDDA removed the Jewels

The Jewels on her breast he took away

And ISHTAR asked

Why, Guardian of the Outer, has thou removed my
Fourth Jewel?

And the Guardian answered

Thus it is, the Covenant of Old, set down before
Time,

The Rules of the Lady of KUTU.

Enter the Fourth Gate.

At the Fifth Gate

NINNGHIZHIDDA removed the Jewels

The Belt of Jewels around her hips he took away

And ISHTAR asked

Why, Watcher of the Forbidden Entrance, hast thou
removed my Fifth Jewel?

And the Watcher answered

Thus it is, the Covenant of Old, set down before Time,
The Rules of the Lady of KUTU.
Enter the Fifth Gate.

At the Sixth Gate
NINNGHIZHIDDA removed the Jewels
The Jewels around her wrists
And the Jewels around her ankles he took away.
And ISHTAR asked
Why, NINNKIGAL, hast thou removed my Sixth Jewel?
And NINNKIGAL answered
Thus it is, the ancient Covenant, set down before Time,
The Decrees of the Lady of KUTU.
Enter the Sixth Gate.

At the Seventh Gate

NINNGHIZHIDDA removed the Jewels
The Jeweled Robes of ISHTAR he took away.
ISHTAR, without protection, without safety,
ISHTAR, without talisman or amulet, asked
Why, Messenger of the Ancient Ones, hast thou removed my Seventh Jewel?
And the Messenger of the Ancient Ones replied
Thus it is, the Covenant of Old, set down before Time,
The Rules of the Lady of KUTU.
Enter the Seventh Gate and behold the Nether World.

ISHTAR has descended to the Land of KUR
To the Depths of CUTHA she went down.
Having lost her Seven Talismans of the Upper Worlds
Having lost her Seven Powers of the Land of the Living
Without Food of Life or Water of Life
She appeared before ERESHKIGAL, Mistress of Death.
ERESHKIGAL screamed at Her presence.

ISHTAR raised up Her arm.
ERESHKIGAL summoned NAMMTAR
The Magician NAMMTAR
Saying these words she spoke to him
Go! Imprison her!
Bind her in Darkness!
Chain her in the Sea below the Seas!
Release against her the Seven ANNUNNAKI!
Release against her the Sixty Demons!
Against her eyes, the demons of the eyes!
Against her sides, the demons of the sides!
Against her heart, the demons of the heart!
Against her feet, the demons of the feet!
Against her head, the demons of the head!
Against her entire body, the demons of KUR!

And the demons tore at her, from every side.

And the ANNUNNAKI, Dread Judges
Seven Lords of the Underworld
Drew Around Her
Faceless Gods of ABSU
They stared
Fixed her with the Eye of Death

With the Glance of Death
They killed her
And hung her like a corpse from a stake
The sixty demons tearing her limbs from her sides
Her eyes from her head
Her ears from her skull.

ERESHKIGAL rejoiced.
Blind AZAG-THOTH rejoiced
IAK SAKKAK rejoiced
ISHNIGGARAB rejoiced
KUTULU rejoiced
The MASKIM gave praise to the Queen of Death
The GIGIM gave praise to ERESHKIGAL, Queen of
    Death.

And the Elder Ones were rent with fear.

Our Father ENKI
Lord of Magick
Receiving word by NINSHUBUR
ISHTAR's servant NINSHUBUR
He hears of ISHTAR's Sleep
In the House of Death
He hears how GANZIR has been
Opened
How the Face of the Abyss
Opened wide its mouth
And swallowed the Queen of Heaven
Queen of the Rising of the Sun.

And ENKI summoned forth clay
And ENKI summoned forth wind

And from the clay and from the wind
ENKI fashioned two Elementals
He fashioned the KURGARRU, spirit of the Earth,
He fashioned the KALATURRU, spirit of the Seas,
To the KURGARRU he gave the Food of Life
To the KALATURRU he gave the Water of Life
And to these images he spoke aloud
Arise, KURGARRU, Spirit of the Earth
Arise, KALATURRU, Spirit of the Seas
Arise, and set thy feet to the Gate GANZIR
To the Gate of the Underworld
The Land of No Return
Set thine eyes
The Seven Gates shall open for thee
No spell shall keep thee out
For my Number is upon you.
Take the bag of the Food of Life
Take the bag of the Water of Life
And ERESHKIGAL shall not harm you
ERESHKIGAL shall not raise her arm against you
ERESHKIGAL SHALL HAVE NO POWER OVER YOU.

Find the corpse of INANNA
Find the corpse of ISHTAR our Queen
And sprinkle the Food of Life, Sixty Times
And sprinkle the Water of Life, Sixty Times
Sixty Times the Food of Life and the Water of Life
Sprinkle upon her body
And truly
ISHTAR will rise.

With giant wings

And scales like serpents
The two elementals flew to the Gate
Invisible
NINNGHIZHIDDA saw them not
Invisible
They passed the Seven Watchers
With haste they entered the Palace of Death
And they beheld several terrible sights.

The demons of all the Abyss lay there
Dead but Dreaming, they clung to the walls
Of the House of Death
Faceless and terrible
The ANNUNNAKI stared out
Blind and Mad AZAG-THOTH reared up
The Eye on the Throne opened
The Dark Waters stirred
The Gates of Lapis Lazuli glistened
In the darkness
Unseen Monsters
Spawned at the Dawn of Ages
Spawned in the Battle of MARDUK and TIAMAT
Spawned by HUBUR
With the Sign of HUBUR
Lead by KINGU . . .

With haste they fled
Through the Palace of Death
Stopping only at the corpse of ISHTAR

The Beautiful Queen
Mistress of the Gods

Lady of all the Harlots of UR
Bright Shining One of the Heavens
Beloved of ENKI
Lay hung and bleeding
From a thousand fatal wounds.

ERESHKIGAL
Sensing their presence
Cried out.

KURGARRU
Armed with Fire
Looked upon the Queen of Corpses
with the Ray of Fire

KALATURRU
Armed with Flame
Looked upon the Queen of the Graves
With the Rays of Flame.

And ERESHKIGAL
Mighty in CUTHA
Turned her face

Upon the corpse of INANNA
Sixty times they sprinkled
The Water of Life of ENKI
Upon the corpse of ISHTAR
Sixty times they sprinkled
The Food of Life of ENKI

Upon the corpse

Hung from a stake
They directed the Spirit of Life

INANNA AROSE.

The Dark Waters trembled and roiled.

AZAG-THOTH screamed upon his throne
CUTHALU lurched forth from his sleep
ISHNIGARRAB fled the Palce of Death
IAK SAKKAK trembled in fear and hate
The ANNUNNAKI fled their thrones
The Eye upon the Throne took flight
ERESHKIGAL roared and summoned NAMMTAR
The Magician NAMMTAR she called
But not for pursuit
But for protection.

INANNA ascended from the Underworld.

With the winged elementals she fled the Gates
Of GANZIR and NETI she fled
And verily
The Dead fled ahead of her.

When through the First Gate they fled
ISHTAR took back her jeweled robes.

When through the Second Gate they fled
ISHTAR took back her jeweled bracelets.

When through the Third Gate they fled
ISHTAR took back her jeweled belt.

When through the Fourth Gate they fled
ISHTAR took back her jeweled necklace.

When through the Fifth Gate they fled
ISHTAR took back her Belt of Jewels.

When through the Sixth Gate they fled
ISHTAR took back her Wand of Lapis.

When through the Seventh Gate they fled
ISHTAR took back her jeweled Crown.

And the Demons rose
And Spirits of the Dead
And went with her out of the Gates
Looking neither right nor left
Walking in front and behind
They went with ISHTAR from the Gate of GANZIR
Out of the Netherworld they accompanied her
And ERESHKIGAL
Scorned Queen of the Abyss Wherein All Are Drowned
Pronounced a Curse
Solemn and Powerful
Against the Queen of the Rising of the Sun
And NAMMTAR gave it form.

When the Lover of ISHTAR
Beloved of the Queen of Heaven
Goes down before me
Goes through the Gate of GANZIR
To the House of Death
When with him the wailing people come

The weeping woman and the wailing man
When DUMUZI is slain and buried
   MAY THE DEAD RISE AND SMELL THE INCENSE!

V

Stoop not down, therefore,
Unto the Darkly Shining World
Where the ABSU lies in Dark Waters
And CUTHALU sleeps and dreams

Stoop not down, therefore,
For an Abyss lies beneath the World
Reached by a descending Ladder
That hath Seven Steps
Reached by a descending Pathway
That hath Seven Gates
And therein is established
The Throne
Of an Evil and Fatal Force.
For from the Cavities of the World
Leaps forth the Evil Demon
The Evil God
The Evil Genius
The Evil Ensnarer
The Evil Phantom
The Evil Devil
The Evil Larvae
Showing no true Signs
Unto mortal Man.
       AND THE DEAD WILL RISE AND
          SMELL THE INCENSE!

The
URILIA
Text

THE following is the Text of URILIA, the Book of the Worm. It contains the formulae by which the wreakers of havoc perform their Rites. These are the prayers of the ensnarers, the liers-in-wait, the blind fiends of Chaos, the most ancient evil.

These incantations are said by the hidden priests and creatures of these powers, defeated by the Elders and the Seven Powers, led by MARDUK, supported by ENKI and the whole Host of IGIGI; defeaters of the Old Serpent, the Ancient Worm, TIAMAT, the ABYSS, also called KUTULU the Corpse-God, slain by the wrath of MARDUK and the Magick of ENKI, yet who lies not dead, but dreaming; he whom secret priests, initiated into the Black Rites, whose names are writ forever in the Book of Chaos, can summon if they but know how.

These words are not to be shown to any man, or the Curse of ENKI be upon thee!

Such are the Words:

IA
IA
IA
IO
IO
IO
I AM the God of Gods
I AM the Lord of Darkness, and Master of Magicians
I AM the Power and the Knowledge
I AM before all things.

I AM before ANU and the IGIGI
I AM before ANU and the ANNUNNAKI
I AM before the Seven SHURUPPAKI
I AM before all things.

I AM before ENKI and SHAMMASH
I AM before all things.

I AM before NINNURSAK and the TABLE of LENKI
I AM before all things.

I AM before INANNA and ISHTAR
I AM before NANNA and UDDU
I AM before ENDUKUGGA and NINDUKUGGA
I AM before ERESHKIGAL
I AM before all things.
Before ME was made Nothing that was made.

I AM before all gods.
I AM before all days.
I AM before all men and legends of men.

I AM the ANCIENT ONE.

NO MAN may seek my resting place.
I receive the Sun at night and the Moon by day.
I AM the receiver of the sacrifice of the Wanderers.
The Mountains of the West cover me.
The Mountains of Magick cover me.

I AM THE ANCIENT OF DAYS.

I AM before ABSU.
I AM before NAR MARRATU.
I AM before ANU.
I AM before KIA.

I AM before all things.

IA! IA! IA! IA SAKKAKTH! IAK SAKKAKH! IA SHA
    XUL!
IA! IA! IA UTUKKU XUL!
IA! IA ZIXUL! IA ZIXUL!
IA KINGU! IA AZBUL! IA AZABUA! IA XAZTUR! IA
    HUBBUR!
IA! IA! IA!
BAXABAXAXAXAXABAXAXAXAXA!
KAKHTAKHTAMON IAS!

II. THE ABOMINATIONS

The terrible offspring of the Ancient Ones may be summoned by the priest. These offspring may be called and adjured to perform what tasks the priest may deem necessary in his temple. They were begotten before all ages and dwelt in the blood of KINGU, and MARDUK could not altogether shut them out. And they dwell in our country, and alongside our generations, though they may not be seen. And this was taught by the priests of Babylon, who charged that these formulae may never be revealed to anyone who is not initiated into our ways, for to do so would be the most frightful error.

Though they dwell beyond the Gate, they may be summoned when MARDUK is not watchful, and sleeps, on those days when he has no power, when the Great Bear hangs from its tail, and on the four quarters of the year computed therefrom, and on the spaces between these Angles. On these days, the Mother TIAMAT is restless, the corpse KUTULU shakes beneath the Earth, and our Master ENKI is sore afraid.

Prepare, then, the bowl of TIAMAT, the DUR of INDUR, the Lost Bowl, the Shattered Bowl of the Sages, summoning thereby the FIRIK of GID, and the Lady SHAKUGUKU, the Queen of the Cauldron. Recite the Conjuration IA ADU EN I over it, and build the Fire therein, calling GBL when thou dost, after his manner and form.

When the Fire is built and conjured, then mayest thou raise thine Dagger, summoning the assistance of NINKHARSAG, Queen of the Demons, and NINKASZI, the Horned Queen, and NINNGHIZHIDDA, the Queen of the Magick Wand, after their manner and form. And when thou hast accomplished this, and made the proper sacrifice, thou mayest begin calling whichsoever of the offspring thou mayest, after opening the Gate.

DO NOT OPEN THE GATE, SAVE FOR AN ESPECIAL TIME THAT THOU STATE AT THE TIME OF OPENING, AND IT MAY NOT STAY OPEN FOR A MOMENT AFTER THE PASSAGE OF THE HOUR OF TIAMAT, ELSE ALL THE ABYSS BREAK FORTH UPON THE EARTH, AND THE DEAD RISE TO EAT THE LIVING, FOR IT IS WRIT: I WILL CAUSE THE DEAD TO RISE AND DEVOUR THE LIVING, I WILL GIVE TO THE DEAD POWER OVER THE LIVING, THAT THEY MAY OUTNUMBER THE LIVING.

After thou hast performed the necessary, called the Spirit, appointed his task, set the time of the closing of the Gate and the return of the Spirit therein, thou must not leave the place of Calling, but remain there until the return of the Spirit and the closing of the Gate.

The Lord of Abominations is HUMWAWA of the South Winds, whose face is a mass of the entrails of the animals and men. His breath is the stench of dung, and no incense can banish the odor from where HUMWAWA has been. HUMWAWA is the Dark Angel of all that is excreted, and of all that sours. And as all things come to the time when they will decay, so also HUMWAWA is the Lord of the Future of all that goes upon the earth, and any man's future years may be seen by gazing into the very face of this Angel, taking care not to breathe the horrid perfume that is the odor of death.

And this is the Signature of HUMWAWA:

And if HUMWAWA appears to the priest, will not the dread PAZUZU also be there? Lord of all fevers and plagues, grinning Dark Angel of the Four Wings, horned, with rotting genitalia, from which he howls in pain through sharpened teeth over the lands of the cities sacred to the APHKHALLU even in the height of the Sun as in the height of the Moon; even with whirling sand and wind, as with empty stillness, and it is the able magician indeed who can remove PAZUZU once he has laid hold of a man, for PAZUZU lays hold unto death.

Know that HUMWAWA and PAZUZU are brothers. HUMWAWA is the eldest, who rides upon a silent, whispering wind and claims the flocks for his own, by which sign you shall know that PAZUZU will come.

And this is the Sigil of PAZUZU by which he is constrained to come:

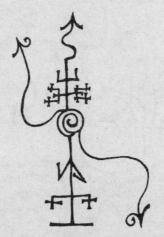

Of all the Gods and Spirits of Abomination, there can be no use or gain to call upon AZAG-THOTH, as he is surely Mad. Rendered sightless in the Battle, he is Lord of CHAOS, and the priest can find little use for him. He is also too powerful to control once called, and gives violent struggle before sent back to the Gate, for which only a strong and able magician may dare raise him. Thus, for that reason, his seal is not given.

Of all the Gods and Spirits of Abomination, KUTULU only cannot be summoned, for he is the Sleeping Lord. The magician can not hope to have any power over him, but he may be worshipped and for him the proper sacrifices may be made, so that he will spare thee when he rises to the earth. And the times for the sacrifice are the same times as the Sleeping of MARDUK, for this is when Great KUTULU moves. And he is the very Fire of the Earth, and Power of All Magick.

When he joins with the Abominations of the Sky, TIAMAT will once more rule the earth!

And this is his Seal:

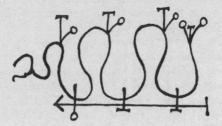

And there are Four Spirits of the Spaces, and hey come upon the Wind, and they are Things of the Vind, and of Fire. And the First comes from the North, i.nd is called USTUR, and has a Human Shape. And He is the Most Ancient of the Four, and a Great Lord of the World. And the Second comes from the East, and is called SED and has the Shape of a Bull, but with a human face, and is very mighty. And the Third comes from the South, and is called LAMAS, and is of the Shape of a Lion, but with a human head, and governs those things of the Flame and the Burning Wind. And the Fourth comes from the West, and is called NATTIG, and is of the Shape of an Eagle, but with a human body, having only the face and wings of an Eagle, with an Eagle's claws. And this Eagle comes from the Sea and is a Great Mystery.

And from Nuzku upon Uru they come, and do not wait, and are always present, and they receive the Wanderers in their Seasons. And the Season of SED is that of the Great Night, when the Bear is slain, and this is in the Month of AIRU. And the Season of LAMAS is the Month of ABU, and that of NATTIG in ARAHSHAMMA and lastly that of USTUR in SHABATU. Thus are the

Four Spirits of the Four Spaces, and their Seasons; and they dwell between the Sun's Spaces, and are not of them, but of the Stars, and, as it is said, of the very IGIGI themselves although this is not altogether known.

And to summon these and other Demons, the herb AGLAOPHOTIS must be burnt in a new bowl that has a crack, and the Incantations recited clearly. And it must be the Evil Times, and at Night.

And the AKHKHARU may be summoned, which sucketh the blood from a Man, as it desires to become a Man, and must take that which MARDUK took in his fashioning of Man, the Blood of KINGU, but the AKHKHARU will never become Man. And the AKHKHARU may be summoned, if its Sign be known, and it is thus:

And the LALASSU may be called, which haunteth the places of Man, seeking also to become like Man, but these are not to be spoken to, lest the Priest become afflicted with madness, and become unto a living LALASSU which must needs be slain and the Spirit thereof exorcised, for it is Evil and causeth only terror, and no good can come of it. It is like the LALARTU, and of the same Family as that, save the LALARTU was once living and is caught between the Worlds, seeking Entrance into one or the other. And it must not be permitted Entrance into This, for it is of a sickened constitution and will slay mothers at birth, like unto LAMASHTA, the Queen of Sickness and Misery.

And the Signs by which these Things may be summoned are these, if the Priest have need of them, but know that it is not lawful:

And this is the Seal of the LALASSU:

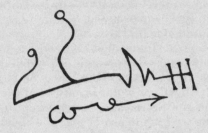

And this is the Seal of the LALARTU:

And know that the MINU of ENKI is powerful against these, but against all Operations of Demonic character, and some of these may be rendered fruitless thereby. Therefore it must always be hid.

Know that GELAL and LILIT are quick to come at Calling, and invadeth the beds of Man, robbing the Water of Life and the Food of Life in which to quicken the Dead, but their labors are fruitless for they do not have the formulae. But the Priest has the formulae, and the Food of Life and the Water of Life may be brought to him by such as these, should he call them. But he must call many, for after the passage of one-tenth of a Moon the Elements are dead.

And GELAL invades the bed of a Woman, and LILIT that of a Man, and sometimes evil beings are born of these hauntings, and as such must be slain, for the children of GELAL are workers natural of the ANCIENT ONE, having His Spirit; and the children of LILIT are likewise, but are born in secret places which may not be perceived by Man, and it is not until the time of their maturity that such as these are given to walking in the places of Men.

And GELAL rideth upon the Wind, but oftentimes LILIT cometh of the Water. Which is why running Water must be used in the Rites, because of the cleanliness thereof.

And the Sign of GELAL is thus:

And the Sign of LILIT is thus:

And XASTUR is a foul demoness who slays Men in their Sleep, and devours that which she will. And of her no more may be said, for it is unlawful; but know that the worshippers of TIAMAT know her well, and that she is beloved of the Ancient Ones.

This is her Sign, by which you may know her:

And know further that the legions of these Evil Ones are uncountable and stretcheth forth on all sides, and into all places, though they cannot be seen, except at certain times and to certain persons. And these times are as said before, and the persons unknown, for who can know XASTUR?

But the Dead may be always summoned, and many times are willing to rise; but some are stubborn and desire to remain Where they are, and do not rise, save for the efforts of the Priest, who has power, as ISHTAR, both in this Place and in the Other. And the Dead must be called in the Four Directions, and in the Four Spaces for, not knowing where It is, the Priest must needs take especial care that he call everywhere, for the Spirit may be in flight.

And a Dead God may be also summoned, and the formulae is that which follows. It must be spoken clearly aloud, and not a word changed, else the Spirit of the God may devour thee, as there is no Food and no Drink where they are.

And it must be called in a secret place, without windows, or with windows only in one place, and that should be in the Northern Wall of the place, and the only light shall be of one lamp, set on the altar, and the lamp need not be new, nor the altar, for it is a Rite of Age and of the Ancient Ones, and they care not for newness.

And the altar should be of a large rock set in the earth, and a sacrifice acceptable unto the nature of the God should be made. And at the time of the Calling, the waters of ABSU will roil, and KUTULU will stir, but unless it be His time, he will not Rise.

And this is the Conjuration of the Dead God:

May NAMMTAR open my eyes that I may see.........
May NAMMTAR open my ears that I may hear.........
May NAMMTAR open my nose that I may sense His approach.
May NAMMTAR open my mouth that my voice will be heard to the far reaches of the Earth.
May NAMMTAR strengthen my right hand that I shall be strong, to keep the Dead......... under my power, under my very power.

I conjure Thee, O Ancestor of the Gods!

I summon Thee, Creature of Darkness, by the Works of Darkness!

I summon Thee, Creature of Hatred, by the Words of Hatred!

I summon Thee, Creature of the Wastes, by the Rites of the Waste!

I summon Thee, Creature of Pain, by the Words of Pain!

I summon and call Thee forth, from Thy Abode in Darkness!

I evoke Thee from Thy resting-place in the bowels of the Earth!

I summon Thine eyes to behold the Brightness of my Wand, which is full of the Fire of Life!

I conjure Thee, O Ancestor of the Gods!

I summon Thee, Creature of Darkness, by the Works of Darkness!

I summon Thee, Creature of Hatred, by the Works of Hatred!

I summon Thee, Creature of the Wastes, by the Rites of the Waste!

I summon Thee, Creature of Pain, by the Words of Pain!

By the Four Square Pillars of Earth that support the Sky,

May they stand fast against Them that desire to harm me!

I evoke Thee from Thy resting-place in the bowels of the Earth!

I summon Thee and Thine ears to hear the Word that is never spoken, except by Thy Father, the Eldest of All Who Know Age

The Word that Binds and Commands is my Word!

IA! IA! IA! NNGI BANNA BARRA IA!
IARRUGISHGARRAGNARAB!

I conjure Thee, O Ancestor of the Gods!

I summon Thee, Creature of Darkness, by the Works of
    Darkness!
I summon Thee, Creature of Hatred, by the Works of
    Hatred!
I summon Thee, Creature of the Wastes, by the Rites of
    the Waste!
I summon Thee, Creature of Pain, by the Words of Pain!

I summon Thee, and call Thee forth, from Thy Abode in
    Darkness!
I evoke Thee from Thy resting-place in the Bowels of the
    Earth!

MAY THE DEAD RISE!

MAY THE DEAD RISE AND SMELL THE INCENSE!

And this shall be recited only once, and if the
God do not appear, do not persist, but finish the Rite
quietly, for it means that It hath been summoned
elsewhere, or is engaged in some Work which it is better
not to disturb.

And when thou hast set out bread for the dead to
eat, remember to pour honey thereupon, for it is pleasing
to the Goddess Whom No One Worshippeth, Who
wanders by night through the streets amid the howling
of the dogs and the wailing of the infants, for in Her time

a great Temple was built unto Her and sacrifices of infants made that She might save the City from the Enemies who dwelt without. And the Number of infants thus slain is countless and unknowable. And She did save that City, but it was taken soon thereafter when the people no more offered up their children. And when the people made to offer again, at the time of the attack, the Goddess turned her back and fled from her temple, and it is no more. And the Name of the Goddess is no more known. And She maketh the infants restless, and to cry, so the reason for the pouring of honey over the sacred bread, for it is written:

Bread of the Cult of the Dead in its Place I eat
In the Court prepared
Water of the Cult of the Dead in its Place I drink
A Queen am I, Who has become estranged to the Cities
She that comes from the Lowlands in a sunken boat
Am I.

I AM THE VIRGIN GODDESS
HOSTILE TO MY CITY
A STRANGER IN MY STREETS.
MUSIGAMENNA URUMA BUR ME YENSULAMU
GIRME EN!
Oh, Spirit, who understand thee? Who comprehend Thee?

Now, there are Two Incantations to the Ancient Ones set down here, which are well known to the Sorcerers of the Night, they who make images and burn them by the Moon and by other Things. And they burn unlawful grasses and herbs, and raise tremendous Evils, and their Words are never written down, it is said. But these are. And they are Prayers of Emptiness and Darkness, which rob the spirit.

Hymn To the Ancient Ones

They are lying down, the Great Old Ones.
The bolts are fallen and the fastenings are placed.
The crowds are quiet and the people are quiet.
The Elder Gods of the Land
The Elder Goddesses of the Land
SHAMMASH
SIN
ADAD
ISHTAR
Have gone to sleep in heaven.
They are not pronouncing judgements.
They are not deciding decisions.
Veiled is the Night.
The Temple and the Most Holy Places are quiet and dark.
The Judge of Truth
The Father of the Fatherless
SHAMMASH
Has gone to his chamber.
O Ancient Ones!
Gods of the Night!
AZABUA!
IAK SAKKAK!
KUTULU!
NINNGHIZHIDDA!
O Bright One, GIBIL!
O Warrior, IRRA!
Seven Stars of Seven Powers!
Ever-Shining Star of the North!
SIRIUS!
DRACONIS!

CAPRICORNUS!
Stand by and accept
This sacrifice I offer
May it be acceptable
To the Most Ancient Gods!

IA MASHMASHTI! KAKAMMU SELAH!

Invocation of the Powers

Spirit of the Earth, Remember!
Spirit of the Seas, Remember!
In the Names of the Most Secret Spirits of NAR
    MARRATUK
The Sea below the seas
And of KUTULU
The Serpent who sleepth Dead
From beyond the graves of the Kings
From beyond the tomb wherein INANNA
Daughter of the Gods
Gained Entrance to the Unholy Slumbers
Of the she-fiend of KUTHULETH

In SHURRUPAK, I summon thee to mine aid!
In UR, I summon thee to mine aid!
In NIPPURR, I summon thee to mine aid!
In ERIDU, I summon thee to mine aid!
In KULLAH, I summon thee to mine aid!
In LAAGASH, I summon thee to mine aid!

Rise up, O powers from the Sea below all seas
From the grave beyond all graves
From the Land of TIL
To SHIN
NEBO
ISHTAR
SHAMMASH
NERGAL
MARDUK
ADAR

House of the Water of Life
Pale ENNKIDU
Hear me!

Spirit of the Seas, Remember!

Spirit of the Graves, Remember!

      And with these incantations, and with others, the sorcerers and the she-sorcerers call many things that harm the life of man. And they fashion images out of wax, and out of flour and honey, and of all the metals, and burn them or otherwise destroy them, and chant the ancient curses, thereby destroying men, cities, and civilizations. And they cause plagues, for they summon PAZUZU. And they cause madness, for they call AZAG-THOTH. And these Spirits come upon the Wind, and some upon the Earth, crawling. And no oil, no powder, suffices to save a man from this inquity, save the exorcisms handed down and recited by the able Priest. And they work by the Moon, and not by the Sun, and by older planets than the Chaldaens were aware. And in cords, they tie knots, and each is a spell. And if these knots be found, they may be untied, and the cords burnt, and the spell shall be broken, as it is written:

AND THEIR SORCERIES SHALL BE AS MOLTEN WAX, AND NO MORE.

And a man may cry out, what have I done, and my generation that such evil shall befall me? And it means nothing, save that a man, being born, is of sadness, for he is of the Blood of the Ancient Ones, but has the Spirit of the Elder Gods breathed into him. And his body goes to the Ancient Ones, but his mind is turned towards the Elder Gods, and this is the War which shall be always fought, unto the last generation of man; for the World is unnatural. When the Great KUTULU rises up and greets the Stars, then the War will be over, and the World be One.

Such is the Covenant of the Abominations and the End of this Text.

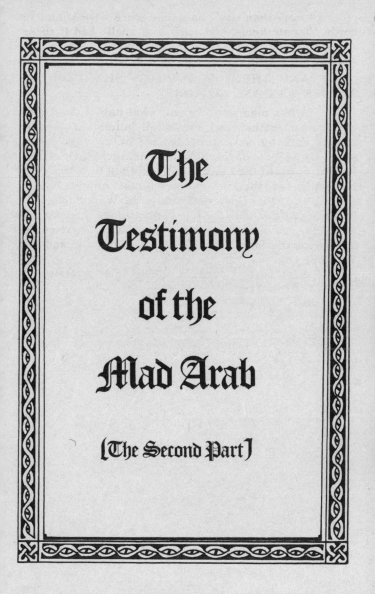

The

Testimony

of the

Mad Arab

[The Second Part]

UR! NIPPUR!
ERIDU! KULLAH!
KESH! LAGASH!
SHURUPPAK SELAH!

Day of Living, Rising Sun
Day of Plenty, gracious Sun
Day of Perfect, Grand Delight
Day of Fortune, Brilliant Night
O Shining Day!
O Laughing Day!
O Day of Life, and Love and Luck!
Seven Oldest, Wisest Ones!
Seven Sacred, Learned Ones!
Be my Guardians, polished Swords
Be my Watchful, patient Lords
Protect me from the Rabishu
O Shining, Splendorous APHKALLHU!

What God have I offended? What Goddess? What sacrifice have I failed to make? What Unknown Evil have I committed, that my going out should be thus accompanied by the fearful howlings of a hundred wolves?

May the heart of my God return to its place!
May the heart of my Goddess return to its place!
May the God I do not know be quieted toward me!

May the Goddess I do not know be quieted toward me!

May the heart of the Unknown God return to its place for me!

May the heart of the Unknown Goddess return to its place for me!

I have traveled on the Spheres, and the Spheres do not protect me. I have descended into the Abyss, and the Abyss does not protect me. I have walked to the tops of mountains, and the mountains do not protect me. I have walked the Seas, and the Seas do not protect me.

The Lords of the Wind rush about me and are angered. The Lords of the Earth crawl about my feet and are angered. The Spirits have forgotten me.

My time is shortened, and I must complete as much as I can before I am taken away by the Voice that ever calls. The Moon's days are numbered upon the earth, and the Sun's, and I know not the meaning of these omens, but that they are. And the oracles are dried up, and the stars spin in their places. And the heavens look to be uncontrolled, with no order, and the spheres are crooked and wandering.

And the Sign of Zdaq is floating above my writing table, but I cannot read the runes any longer, for that Sight is failing me. Is it always in this fashion? And the Sign of Xastur rises up behind me, and of that I know the meaning, but may not write, for I received the message Elsewhere.

I can hardly speak to recognize my own voice.

The Abyss yawns wide before me! A Gate has been broken!

Know that the Seven Spheres must be entered in their times and in their seasons, one at a time, and never the one before the other. Know that the Four Beasts of the Spaces claim the blood of the initiate, each in their own time and season. Know that TIAMAT seeks ever to rise to the stars, and when the Upper is united to the Lower, then a new Age will come of Earth, and the Serpent shall be made whole, and the Waters will be as One, when on high the heavens had not been named.

Remember to protect the livestock of the village and thy family. The Elder Sign and the Sign of the Race. But the Watcher, too, if They be slow. And no sacrifices are to be made in that time, for the blood will be spilt for them that have come in, and will call them.

Remember to keep to the low ground, and not the high, for the Ancient Ones swing easily to the tops of the temples and the mountains, whereby they may survey what they had lost the last time. And sacrifices made on the tops of those temples are lost to Them.

Remember thy life is in running water, and not in still water, for the latter is the breeding place of the LILITU, and her creatures are the offspring of Them, and do worship at Their shrines, the places of which are unknown to thee. But where thou seest a standing stone, there they will be, for such is their altar.

Remember to carve the signs exactly as I have told thee, changing not one mark lest the amulet prove a curse against thee that wear it. Know that salt absorbs the evil effluvia of the larvae, and is useful to cleanse the tools with. Do not speak first to the demon, but let him speak first to thee. And if he speak, charge him to speak clearly, in a soft and pleasing voice, and in thy tongue, for it will otherwise surely confuse thee and deafen thee with its roar. And charge it to keep its stench that it may not make thee faint.

Remember not to make the sacrifice either too large or too small, for if it is too small, the demon will not come or, if coming, will be angered with thee so that it will not speak, even when charged, for that is the Covenant. And if it be too large, it will grow too large and too fast and will become difficult to control. And one such demon was raised by that Priest of Jerusalem, ABDUL BEN-MARTU, and was fed extensively on the sheep of the flocks of Palestine, whereupon it grew to frightening proportion and eventually devoured him. But that was madness, for Ben-Martu worshipped the Old Ones, which is unlawful, as it is written.

Remember that the Essences of the Ancient Ones are in all things, but that the Essences of the Elder Gods are in all things that live, and this will prove of value to thee when the time comes.

Remember the ARRA, especially when dealing with Them of Fire, for They respect it, and no other.

Remember to keep the Moon pure.

Beware of the Cults of Death, and these are the Cult of the Dog, the Cult of the Dragon, and the Cult of the Goat; for they are worshippers of the Ancient Ones, and forever try to let Them in, for they have a formula of which it is unlawful to speak. And these cults are not strong, save at their seasons, when the heavens open up to them and unto their race. And there shall forever be War between us and the Race of Draconis, for the Race of Draconis was ever powerful in ancient times, when the first temples were built in MAGAN, and they drew down much strength from the stars, but now they are as Wanderers of the Wastelands, and dwell in caves and in deserts, and in all lonely places where they have set up stones. And these I have seen, in my journeys through those areas where the ancient cults once flourished, and where now there is only sadness and desolation.

And I have seen them in their Rites, and the awful Things they call forth from the Lands beyond Time. I have seen the Signs carved upon their stones, their altars. I have seen the Signs of PAZUZU, and ZALED, and those of XASTUR and AZAG-THOTH, and similarly those of ISHNIGARRAB and the awful

Offspring of the Goat, and the terrible musicks of their Race.

I have seen the Blood spilt upon the Stone. I have seen that Stone struck with a Sword, and have seen the Stone raise up and the Serpent crawl forth. And this power is surely damned; but where does MARDUK tarry? And what of SHAMMASH? The Sleeping Gods truly Sleep.

And what crime have I committed? What Unknown God have I transgressed? What forbidden thing have I eaten? What forbidden thing have I drunk? My suffering! It is Seven! It is Seven times Seven! O Gods! Do not cast thy servant down!

Remember the Scorpion Man who dwells in the Mountains. He was of old created by TIAMAT to fight the Elder Gods, but was permitted to stay below the Mountains by Them. But He has deceived us once, and may do so again. But call upon him if there be something concerning the Outside that you would know, that I have not told thee. And his sign is simple, and it is thus:

And merely, face the place where he is, and he will come and speak, but do not do this at Dawn, for then the Sun rises and the Scorpion has no power, not from the Dawn till the Dusk, during which time he is forced back beneath the Earth, for that is the letter of the Covenant concerning him, for it is written: He shall not raise his head above the Sun.

And again: His is the dark times.

And again: He knows of the Gate, but not the Gate.

And the Scorpion Man has another of his Race, female, that dwells with him there, but of her it is not lawful to speak, and she must be banished with the exorcisms should she appear to thee, for her touch is Death.

And of the Cult of the Dragon, what more can I say to thee? They worship when that Star is highest in the heavens, and is of the Sphere of the IGIGI, as are the Stars of the Dog and the Goat. And their worshippers have always been with us, though they are not of our same Race, but of the Race of their Stars, of the Ancient Ones. And they keep not to our laws, but murder quickly, and without thought. And their blood covers them.

They have summoned the Spirits of War and Plague openly upon our Race, and have caused great numbers of our people and our animals to die, after a most unnatural fashion. And they are unfeeling towards pain, and fear not the Sword or the Flame, for they are the authors of all Pain! They are the very creatures of Darkness and Sorrow, yet they Sorrow not! Remember the smell! They can be told by their smell! And their many unnatural sciences and arts, which cause wonderous things to happen, but which are unlawful to our people.

And who is their Master? Of this I do not know, but I have heard them calling ENKI which is surely a blasphemy, for ENKI is of our Race as it is writ in the Text of MAGAN. But, perhaps, they called Another, whose Name I do not know. But surely it was not ENKI.

And I have heard them calling all the Names of the Ancient Ones, proudly, at their Rites. And I have seen the blood spilt upon the ground and the mad dancing and the terrible cries as they yelled upon their Gods to appear and aid them in their mysteries.

And I have seen them turn the very Moon's rays into liquid, the which they poured upon their stones for a purpose I could not divine.

And I have seen them turn into many strange kinds of beast as they gathered in their appointed places, the Temples of Offal, whereupon horns grew from heads that had not horns, and teeth from mouths that had not such teeth, and hands become as the talons of eagles or the claws of dogs that roam the desert areas, mad and howling, like unto those who even now call my name outside this room!

I cry laments, but no one hears me! I am overwhelmed with horror! I cannot see! Gods, do not cast thy servant down!

Remember the Sword of the Watcher. Do not touch It until you want It to depart, for It will depart at a touch and leave thee unprotected for the remainder of the Rite, and although the Circle is a boundary which none can cross, thou wilt find thyself unprepared to meet the incredible sights that will greet thee outside.

Remember also the sacrifices to the Watcher. They must be regular, for the Watcher is of a different Race and cares not for thy life, save that he obey thy commands when the sacrifices have been met.

And forgetting the Elder Sign will surely cause thee much grief.

And I have seen a Race of Man that worships a Giant Cow. And they come from somewhere East, beyond the Mountains. And they are surely worshippers of an Ancient One, but of its Name I am not certain, and do not write it down, for it is useless to thee anyway. And in their Rites, they become as cows, and it is disgusting to see. But they are Evil, and so I warn thee.

And I have seen Rites that can kill a man at a great distance. And Rites that can cause sickness to a man, wherever he lives, by the use of a simple charm, which must be spoken in its tongue and in no other, or so it is said. And this charm is as follows:

> AZAG galra sagbi mu unna te
> NAMTAR galra zibi mu unna te
> UTUK XUL gubi mu unna te
> ALA XUL gabi mu unna te
> GIDIM XUL ibbi mu unna te
> GALLA XUL kadbi mu unna te
> DINGIR XUL girbi mu unna te
> I minabi-ene tashbi aba-andibbi-esh!

And this they would chant over a doll of wax as it was burning in their wicked cauldrons. And in these things they took great delight, and still do where they are to be found at their shrines of loathsomeness.

And I have seen the lands of farmers ravaged by their evil spells, scorched black by flame and burning embers that descend from the sky. And that is the Sign that they have been there, where the earth is black and charred, and where nothing grows.

And when fire comes from the heavens, there wilt surely be panic among the people, and the Priest must calm them and take this book, of which he must make a copy in his own hand, and read the exorcisms therein that his people may not be harmed. For a sword will appear in the sky at those times, a signal to the Ancient Ones that One of Theirs has escaped and entered into this World. And it shall be an omen to thee that such a Spirit is abroad in the land, and must be found. And thou mayest send thy Watcher to the search, and it will surely tell thee of Its neighborhood. And if it is not stopped by the magickal power of the Priest, there will be great destruction of cities, and fire will rain from the spheres, until the Elder Gods see your plight and will quell the uprising of the Ancient Ones with powerful Charms. But many will be lost to the Outside at that time.

Watch well the Stars. For when comets are to be seen in the neighborhood of CAPRICORNUS, His cults will rejoice and the spells will increase from their quarter. And when comets are to be seen in DRACONIS, there is great danger, for the Cults of the Dragon do rise up at that time, and make many sacrifices, not only of animals, but of men.

And when comets are to be seen in the neighborhood of the Star SIRIUS, then there will be great difficulty in the houses of kings, and brother will rise up against brother, and there shall be war and famine. And in these things the worshippers of the Dog will rejoice, and reap the spoils of these conflicts, and will grow fat.

If thou happenest upon such a Cult in the midst of their Rituals, do but hide well so that they do not see thee, else they will surely kill thee and make of thee a sacrifice to their Gods, and thy spirit will be in grave danger, and the howling of the wolves will be for thee and the spirit which escapes from thee. This, if thou be lucky to die quickly, for these Cults rejoice in the slow spilling of blood, whereby they derive much power and strength in their Ceremonies.

Watch well, however, all that they do and all that they say, and write it down in a book that no one will see, as I have done, for it will serve thee well at some future time when thou wilt recognize them by their words or by their actions. And thou mayest procure amulets against them, by which their spells are rendered useless and dull, by burning the Names of their Gods upon parchment or silk in a cauldron of thine own devising. And thy Watcher will carry the burnt spell to their altar and deposit it thereupon, and they will be much afraid and cease their workings for awhile, and their stones will crack and their Gods be sorely angry with their servants.

Write the book thou keepest well, and clearly, and when it is time for thee to go out, as it is my time now, it will pass into the hands of those who may have the best use of it, and who are faithful servants of the Elder Gods, and wilt swear eternal Warfare against the rebellious demons who would destroy the civilizations of man.

And if thou knowest the names of they who would harm thee, write them upon figures of wax, made in their image, upon which you will make the Curse and melt them in the cauldron you have set up within the MANDAL of protection. And the Watcher will carry the Curse to them for whom it was uttered. And they will die.

And if thou dost not know of their names, nor of their persons, save that they seek to harm thee, make a doll of wax like a man, with his limbs, but with no face. And upon the face of the doll write the word KASHSHAPTI. Hold the doll over the flaming cauldron while saying fiercely over it:

ATTI MANNU KASHSHAPTU SHA TUYUB TA ENNI!

and then drop the doll into the flames. From the smoke that rises from this action, you will see the name of the sorcerer or sorceress written within it. And then you will be able to send the Watcher to bring the Curse. And that person will die.

Or thou mayest call upon ISHTAR to protect thee from the spells of sorcery. And for this, the MANDAL must be prepared as always, and a figure of ISHTAR be upon the altar, and incantations made to summon Her assistance, like the following incantation that is ancient, from the Priests of UR:

WHO ART THOU, O WITCH, THAT SEEKEST ME?
Thou hast taken the road
Thou hast come after me
Thou hast sought me continually for my destruction
Thou hast continually plotted an evil thing against me
Thou hast encompassed me
Thou hast sought me out
Thou hast gone forth and followed my steps

But I, by the command of the Queen ISHTAR
Am clothed in terror
Am armed in fiercesomeness
Am arrayed with might and the Sword
I make thee tremble
I make thee run afraid
I drive thee out
I spy thee out
I cause thy name to be known among men
I cause they house to be seen among men
I cause thy spells to be heard among men

I cause thy evil perfumes to be smelt among men
I unclothe thy wickedness and evil
And bring your sorceries to naught!

It is not I, but NANAKANISURRA
Mistress of Witches
And the Queen of Heaven ISHTAR
Who command thee!

And if these worshippers and sorcerers still
come at thee, as it is possible, for their power comes
from the Stars, and who knows the ways of the Stars?,
thou must call upon the Queen of Mysteries,
NINDINUGGA, who wilt surely save thee. And thou must
make incantations with her Title, which is NINDINUG-
GA NIMSHIMSHARGAL ENLILLARA. And it is enough
merely to shout that Name aloud, Seven times, and she
will come to thine aid.

And remember that thou purify thy temple with
the branches of cypress and of pine, and no evil spirit
which haunteth buildings will cause habitation to be set
up therein, and no larvae will breed, as they do in many
unclean places. The larvae are enormous, twice as large
as a man, but do breed on his excretions, and even, it is
said, upon his breath, and grow to terrible height, and do
not leave him until the Priest or some magician cut him
off with the copper dagger, saying the name of ISHTAR
seven times seven times, aloud, in a sharp voice.

The night has now grown silent. The howling of
the wolves has grown quiet, and can scarce be heard.
Perhaps it was some other that they sought? Yet, can I
tell in my bones that this is not so? For the XASTUR sign
has not left its station behind me, and has grown larger,
casting a shadow over these pages as I write. I have

summoned my Watcher, but It is troubled by some Thing and does not respond to me well, as though afflicted with some disease, and dazed.

My books have lost light, and settle upon their shelves like animals fallen asleep, or dead. I am sickened by what voices I hear now, as though the voices of my family, left behind me so many years ago, that it is impossible to conceive that they are about. Did I not understand of their untimely, unnatural death? Can the demons who wait Without take on so viciously the human voices of my parents? My brother? My sister?

AVAUNT THEE!

That this Book were an amulet, a Seal of Protection! That my ink were the ink of Gods and not of Men! But I must write hastily, and if thou cannot read nor understand this writing, perhaps it is sign enough for thee of the strength and power of the demons that be, in these times and in these places, and is surely a warning to thee to have a care and not to invoke carelessly, but cautiously, and not, under any circumstances, seek carelessly to open that Gate to the Outside, for thou can never know the Seasons of Times of the Ancient Ones, even though thou can tell their Seasons upon the Earth by the rules I have already instructed thee to compute; for their Times and Seasons Outside run uneven and strange to our minds, for are they not the Computors of All Time? Did They not set Time in its Place? It were not enough that the Elder Gods (have mercy on Thy servant!) set the Wanderers to mark their spaces, for such spaces as existed were the work of the Ancient Ones. Were no Sun to shine, were SHAMMASH never born, would not the years pass by, as quickly?

Seek ever to keep the Outside Gate closed and sealed, by the instructions I have given thee, by the Seals and the Names herein.

Seek ever to hold back the Powers of the Cults of the ancient Worship, that they might not grow strong on their spilt blood, and on their sacrifice. By their wounds shall ye know them, and by their smell, for they are not born as men, but in some other fashion; by some corruption of seed or spirit that has given them other properties than those we are familiar with. And they like the Dark Places best; for their God is a Worm.

IA! SHADDUYA IA! BARRA! BARRA! IA KANPA! IA KANPA!
ISHNIGARRAB! IA! NNGI IA! IA!

The Stars grow dim in their places, and the Moon pales before me, as though a Veil were blown across its flame. Dog-faced demons approach the circumference of my sanctuary. Strange lines appear carved on my door and walls, and the light from the Window grows increasing dim.
A wind has risen.
The Dark Waters stir.
This is the Book of the Servant of the Gods...

The End of the Book
NECRONOMICON

"Stoop not down, therefore,
Unto the Darkly-Splendid World,
Wherein continually lieth a faithless Depth
And Hades wrapped in clouds,
Delighting in unintelligible images
Precipitous, winding,
A black, ever-rolling Abyss
Ever espousing a Body unluminous
Formless
And Void."

The Chaldean Oracles of Zoroaster